CHRISTIANITY: BEHAVIOUR, ATTITUDES & LIFESTYLES

Foundation Edition

Joanne Cleave

www.heinemann.co.uk
✓ Free online support
✓ Useful weblinks
✓ 24 hour online ordering

01865 888058

Heinemann Educational Publishers
Halley Court, Jordan Hill, Oxford OX2 8EJ
Part of Harcourt Education

Heinemann is the registered trademark of
Harcourt Education Limited

© Joanne Cleave, 2004

First published 2004

08 07 06 05 04
10 9 8 7 6 5 4 3 2 1

British Library Cataloguing in Publication Data is
available from the British Library on request.

ISBN 0 435 30714 2

Copyright notice

Designed and typeset by Artistix, Thame, Oxon

Original illustrations © Harcourt Education Limited,
2003

Illustrated by Andrew Skilleter

Cover design by Artistix, Thame, Oxon

Printed in Spain by Mateu Cromo S.A.

Cover photo: © Magnum Photos

Picture research by Sue Sharp

Acknowledgements
Foundation series consultant: Anne Geldart

The publisher and author would like to thank the following
for permission to reproduce copyright material:

Photographs – p.4 Science Photo Library; pp.5, 20, 21,
61, 83, 90 (bottom right), 100, 116, 126, 130, 132 (top)
Andes Press Agency/Carlos Reyes-Manzo; p.8 (left)
Science Photo Library/Nasa; p.8 (background) Andes
Press Agency/Matt Bryant; p.8 (bottom right) Still Pictures/
Paul Glendell; p.8 (middle) Hutchison Library/ V. Ivleva;
pp.8 (top right), 11 (right), 44, 68, 69, 71 (top right), 103
(top and bottom) Rex Features/Sipa; pp.10, 26, 90 (top
left), 91, 93 John Birdsall; p.11 (left) Still Pictures/Pierre
Gleizes; p.22 Wellcome Picture Library; p.24 Still
Pictures/Reinhard-Janke; pp.32, 40, 132 (bottom) Mirror
Syndication; pp.36 (left and right), 37 (bottom and top)
Circa/Jed Murray; p.42 Getty Images; p.46 Rex
Features/Gerry Gropp; p.56 (bottom) Still Pictures/Mike
Schroder; pp.56 (top) 77, 79, 88, 95, 122 Associated
Press; pp.70, 71 (top left), 76 Mary Evans Picture Library;
p.71 (bottom) Rex Features/Sipa Herb Swanson; p.72 Still
Pictures/John Isaac; 73 (top) Still Pictures/Harmut
Schwarzbach; p.73 (bottom) Rex Features/Ian Back; p.74
Rex Features/Thomas Haley/Sipa; p.78 Press Association;
pp.80, 97 Rex Features; pp.81, 98 Rex Features/Tim
Rooke; p.82 Rex Features/Thomas Haley; p.90 (top right)
Nick Rose; p.90 (bottom left) Hutchison Library/Philip
Wolmuth; p.90 (top middle) Rex Features/Lehtikuva Oy;
p.92 Impact Photos; p.101 Rex Features/Sipa Ron
Hussey; p.102 Bettman/Corbis; p.114 Photodisc; p.115
Hutchison Library; p.125 (top and bottom) Antonia
Cabral/CAFOD; p.133 source unknown; p.135 Hutchison
Library/Tony Souter.

Exam questions – p.14 NEAB 2000, A2; pp.14, 30, 52,
66, 88 AQA 2003; pp.30, 52, 88, 140 NEAB 2000;
pp.52, 140 NEAB 1999; pp.66, 108, 140 AQA 2002;
p.140 NEAB 1997, NEAB and AQA questions reproduced
by permission of the Assessment and Qualifications
Alliance.

Other – The slogans on pp.7, 9, 14, 78, 101 © Trend
Enterprises, Inc; the leaflet extraction p.23 © Exit; the
Amnesty International logo on p.60 © Amnesty International
Publications, 1 Easton Street, London, WC1X 0DW, UK;
the CND logo on p.83 © CND; the leaflet on p.121 ©
Tearfund; the Tearfund logo on p.124 © Tearfund; the
CAFOD logo on p.124 © CAFOD; the Christian Aid logo
on p.126 © Christian Aid; the Trócaire campaign logos on
p.127 © Trócaire; the leaflet on p.128 © Oxfam; The
Children's Society logo on p.134 © The Children's
Society; the NSPCC logo on p.134 © NSPCC; the
Salvation Army logo on p.135 © Salvation Army.

Every effort has been made to contact copyright holders
of material reproduced in this book. Any omissions will be
rectified in subsequent printings if notice is given to the
publishers.

Contents

Notes for teachers

About the book

This book is designed to support AQA's GCSE specification A for Religious Studies, option 2A – Effects of Christianity on behaviour, attitudes and lifestyle. The book is divided into the following sections.

Decisions on life and living:

- the environment
- abortion and voluntary euthanasia
- marriage and relationships.

Justice and reconciliation:

- love and forgiveness
- war and peace.

Christian responsibility:

- prejudice and discrimination
- aid for developing countries.

These sections are divided into topics containing activities and key points that help to consolidate learning. Set Bible passages are from the New International Version (NIV) and appear at the end of the sections to which they are relevant. These are followed by explanatory notes. Please note, some passages have been simplified for easier reading.

At the end of each section there are exam question hints. Support for coursework is also provided.

Key terms are explained the first time they appear. Other difficult words and phrases are found in the glossary and are bold the first time they appear in a section.

Activities

Activities are designed to develop knowledge and understanding of the specification content, and can also be used to develop Key Skills (they are coded to show which Key Skill they might develop). Skills used include the following.

- Research. This can be undertaken on the Internet, in libraries and with classroom-provided resources.
- Discuss. This can be in groups or pairs. More personal issues may be better discussed in groups.
- Group tasks. Ideally, groups should comprise four to six pupils.
- Drama/role-play. Allow time to practise, then perform.
- Explain. This may be explaining a sentence, a word, a phrase or an idea.

Activities are designed to provide active involvement for those pupils for whom a written response would not be their first choice of task. It is an opportunity to get away from pen and paper and do something different.

Common errors

Below are some common errors that students make in this subject.

- They use the word 'vowel' instead of 'vow'.
- They are confused between 'capital' and 'corporal' punishment, between 'abortion' and 'voluntary euthanasia' and between 'abortion' and 'contraception'.
- They hold the incorrect belief that if you are widowed you need a divorce to marry.
- They hold the incorrect belief that in non-violent protests nobody gets hurt.
- They believe, wrongly, that Jesus taught that no one should be punished, only forgiven.
- There is a wrong belief that just war has no killing or violence.
- Many students think 'Love your neighbour' is one of the Ten Commandments.

Notes for students

About your AQA course

This book supports AQA's GCSE Specification A for Religious Studies, option 2A – Effects of Christianity on behaviour, attitudes and lifestyles. In this option, you will look at an issue, then consider different viewpoints, both Christian and non-Christian.

About the book

This book has seven sections each divided into topics. At the beginning of many of the topics you will find key terms. These are words you need to learn. Other difficult words and phrases are in the glossary (pages 145–148). They are printed in bold the first time they appear in a section.

Each topic ends with a summary of the key points. Then there are Activities. These are for you to use skills, such as using research, discussions and role-play.

You will find the set Bible passages, with explanations, at the end of each section. You need to learn the set passages, as there may be questions about any of them.

At the end of each section you will find Exam questions to practise, with hints on how to score full marks.

Issues

'Issues' in this book mean the problems that people face in their lives. Here are some examples.

- Should I have an abortion?
- Should I have sex outside marriage?
- Should I forgive my friend?

Not everybody will agree on the answers. This book gives you several Christian points of view and Bible passages to use for guidance. You need to respect the opinions of others in your groups – even if you feel they are totally wrong.

The Bible

The part of the Bible that Christians call the Old Testament is the Hebrew Bible. People wrote this during a period of 1000 years, but it covers Jewish history back to the beginning. The New Testament took about 100 years to complete. The Gospel writers recorded Jesus' teaching, and showed how he changed the accepted Jewish attitude to the Law.

Some tips!

- Evaluation questions usually begin with a statement, followed by the question 'Do you agree?' Then there is an instruction to give more than one point of view. You will lose marks if you fail to show you know of more than one point of view.

- If the question tells you to use a Bible passage, then you must do so.

- Keep up to date with world affairs that you could use in your coursework or refer to in an answer. Cut out newspaper articles and file them. This could be about wars, natural disasters or human-interest articles.

Decisions on life and living: the environment

In the 1970s, people began to be aware of green issues. These issues include cutting down forests, using up resources such as gas and coal; pollution and the hole in the ozone layer. Adults began to worry about children's health. For example, each year there is an increase in infant asthma and chest infections. This section has information about all these things, and about how Christians can respond and what needs to be done.

This section includes:

- The Bible and science
- Science and creation
- Stewardship
- What is happening to the world?
- What can we do about the world?
- Bible passages
- Exam questions to practise

The Bible and science

Genesis 1 tells a creation story that tries to explain *why* God created the world. It does not attempt to say *how* the world was created. Scientists and others may argue 'Can you be a Christian if you do not believe in Genesis?' However, even scientists cannot agree among themselves about how the world was made.

The creation story

Genesis 1: 1–2: 3 is the main set passage for the **environment** topic. The key points of the passage are outlined below.

In the beginning when God created the universe, the earth was formless and **desolate**.

Day 1: God created light and darkness, called day and night. God saw that it was good.

Day 2: God separated water from the earth and called the dome sky. God saw that it was good.

Day 3: God created the land and the sea, then plants and trees. God saw that it was good.

Day 4: God created the sun, moon and stars to show time and seasons. God saw that it was good.

Day 5: God created the sea monsters, fish and birds. God saw that it was good.

Day 6: God created domestic and wild animals. Then God made humans. God made humans in his image to rule over the world. God saw that it was good.

Day 7: God had finished his work so he made the day holy and rested.

Can Genesis be true?

Darwin's theory of **evolution** states that humans may have evolved from earlier life forms. Some people argue that this means Genesis cannot be 'true' in a scientific sense.

Different opinions

- **Literalists** are Christians who believe events in Genesis happened exactly as written.

- Some people who study languages point out that the Hebrew word that has been translated as 'day' in fact means 'a period of time'.

- Some Christians believe the story is a **myth** which makes it clear that God made the world and *why* he did it, not *how* he did it.

- There are some scientists who say that the Genesis order of creation is basically correct, but it was never intended to be a scientific story.

- Many Christians state that the Genesis story is timeless; it will never be out of date. The writer probably wrote this up to 4000 years ago and definitely did not have scientists, geologists, and twenty-first century technology. The picture on page 3 shows what people thought about the world.

- Some experts point out that the Genesis story is very similar to a creation story told in ancient Babylon. Other stories from Genesis such as the Great Flood and the Tower of Babel are similar too. This should not surprise us. The early Jewish tribes lived and travelled in Babylonia.

The ancient Jewish view of the world.

Activities

1 Use the Internet, or books to find out other ancient creation stories. You may need some help finding out the names of ancient countries. Egypt is one to help you get started. **IT 1.1, C 1.2**

2 Now try to find some other stories such as the Flood. You can write out one story each and read it to the rest of your group. Then you could make a wall display. **IT 1.2**

Key points

- The Genesis story tells its readers that God made humans like him and they were important.

- The early Christians who drew together the **fundamental** (basic) Christian beliefs thought that belief in God the Creator was very important – it is placed first in the **creeds**.

Science and creation

Key terms

Theory of evolution Argues that species gradually evolved from earlier forms.

The big question

Scientists have written many theories about creation. But no sooner is one idea put forward than another is presented. All the theories are based on evidence.

The Big Bang

Many scientists now agree on the **Big Bang theory**. This says there was a huge explosion, when gases blew up and formed planets. 'Where did these gases come from?' is the next big question.

How did life begin?

Some scientists study how life began. They use **fossils** to show that life began in water. They say that minute life forms evolved into different species of fish, birds, reptiles and mammals – including humans.

The Big Bang.

Survival of the fittest

This is part of the **Theory of evolution**. This means that only the animals that adapt to their environment or climate will survive. For example, some animals need to run quickly to avoid being eaten by other animals. The slow ones do not survive. So being able to run fast evolves into a characteristic of that animal.

Humans

There are different opinions about how humans evolved. One theory is that water animals learned to breathe on land and slowly the first humans came. Others say humans came from apes.

Evidence

The human foetus at six weeks in pregnancy has gills that seal over. A human foetus at about five to seven weeks has a tail which is absorbed during pregnancy. Humans have an appendix that they do not need. They also have wisdom teeth they do not need.

Science and Christianity

There are several questions (and answers) about science and Christianity. Here are some of them.

Q: Can I believe in evolution *and* be a Christian?

A: Many would say yes, God is behind evolution.

Q: What is important in all these ideas?

A: God created the world and everything in it. So he may well have used evolution as part of his plan.

Q: What does the **Nicene Creed** say about all this?

A: 'We believe in One God, the Father, the Almighty, maker of heaven and earth, of all that is seen and unseen.'

People in church saying the Creed.

Activities

1 Can you be a Christian *and* believe in evolution? Discuss in groups or as a class. **C 1.1, 2.1a**

2 You are going to find out some information using the Internet or books in the library.
   a Find out more about the Big Bang idea.
   b Find out more about Charles Darwin and evolution. **IT 1.1, 1.2**

Key points

- For many Christians the importance of the Genesis creation story is not whether it is scientifically correct, but that it teaches that God made the world.

- Many Christians would have no doubt that it is perfectly possible to be a Christian *and* accept a scientific theory.

Stewardship

Key terms

Stewardship Looking after something for its owner. Here, it means looking after the world for God.

Green issues Issues about caring for the world.

Conservation Looking after the environment and stopping the harm to the world. Can also mean clearing up the mess.

What is stewardship?

If you look after something for someone, you must take care of it because you know that you must give it back in good condition. Here are some examples of **stewardship**.

- Your dad borrows your granddad's electric hedge trimmer. How would your granddad feel if it was returned blunt and dirty with the plug hanging off?

- You have lent ten pages of physics notes to a friend to copy up before the GCSE exam. How would you feel if that friend returned five pages, the rest scrumpled up, stained with coffee?

If something does not belong to you, you cannot do what you like to it.

Christian stewardship

Christian stewardship is about looking after the world for God. Christians believe that Genesis 1: 22–30 are important verses:

> God said to [the humans], 'Be fruitful and increase in number; fill the earth and subdue it. Rule over the fish of the sea and the birds of the air, over the livestock, over all the earth, and over all the creatures that move along the ground.' Then God said,

> 'I give you every seed-bearing plant on the face of the earth and every tree that has fruit with seed in it. They will be yours for food.'

Many Christians see the idea of stewardship here – God told humans to take care of the world for him. They believe that everyone should care for the world, not just Christians.

Who is guilty?

Christians did not set a good example in the past. Many landowners planted tea and coffee to sell in the West while their villagers starved. Industrial nations destroyed land in their search for minerals such as coal, gold and copper. And this still goes on!

All change!

In the 1970s many people, not just scientists, began to be concerned about the world. They became involved in **green issues**. They began to realize that when some resources, such as coal, have been used up, they cannot be replaced. If an animal becomes **extinct**, it cannot be re-created.

Teen talk

Look at this T-shirt. The slogan was written by Professor Olav, who studies glaciers. When you read the slogan what are your first thoughts? When you had thought about it did your thoughts change? Do you think the slogan is true?

Seen on a teenager's T-shirt in a church.

Technology

There is hope! People have the knowledge and technology to try to put some things right. They can ban the use of **CFCs**, which damage the earth's atmosphere. They can also stop chemical waste being dumped in the sea.

Bible rules, OK

God gave rules to humans about managing the environment. The passage from Exodus on page 13 shows that farmers should let the land lie fallow for a year so that the soil can recover. **Organic farmers** use this idea today. Deuteronomy 20: 19 states:

> When you are trying to capture a city, do not cut down its fruit-trees, even though the siege lasts a long time. Eat the fruit but do not destroy the trees; the trees are not your enemies.

This reminds humans that war destroys the environment.

A Rocha: Christians and conservation

Peter Harris and a group of Christian bird-watchers set up A Rocha. This is an international **conservation** group. They wanted to stop the destruction of marshland with rare birds and other wildlife in Portugal.

Peter and his group built a house with offices and rooms for a vet. Bird watchers stayed there and used hides to watch the birds. Many helped by tagging birds and recording data. Experts joined the team. Churches in the UK provided funds for the project.

British universities and scientists became involved and the project grew. Soon there were similar centres around the world. Local people gave their ideas, and important research began.

Why Christians should get involved in green issues

- God made the world and he cares for it.

- Christians obey God's wish that humans rule the world as sensible stewards.

- The poor suffer most. Natural disasters hit them hardest as they live in the worst housing in every country in the world. This is unjust.

- Many people wonder if there is anything they can do to save the world. The Bible says God will bring harmony if people pray and work for it.

Activities

Read this saying used by Native Americans?

> Only after the last tree
> has been cut down
> Only after the last river
> has been poisoned
> Only after the last fish
> has been caught,
> Only then will you find that
> money cannot be eaten.

a Do you think it is true? List your reasons.
b EITHER design the background to this saying, then add the words and make it into a large poster. OR write your own saying about any green issue that is important to you. **PS 1.2, WO 2.3**

Key points

- Christians believe God made the world, put humans in it and provided for their needs, such as food.

- Christians believe that humans must look after the world on behalf of God.

- It is only recently that people have begun to worry about the world.

What is happening to the world?

Key terms

Extinct Species or sub-species (when referring to wildlife, plants and trees) that has died. There are no more left.

The world today. What can we do to improve things?

So what is happening?

Lack of respect for the world is catching up with us in many ways.

- Every day at least one species of animal, insect, plant or tree becomes extinct.

- Rainforests are the earth's main supply of oxygen. Most rainforests are in South America. Every day whole areas of rainforest are dug up, ploughed or set on fire, to graze cattle, to build new towns or roads and to lay pipelines.

- The ozone layer protects the earth from dangerous sun rays. **Pollution** from CFCs in spray cans and chemical waste have caused a hole in the ozone layer. This has resulted in a rise in skin cancer and other health problems.

- The greenhouse effect means there is a rise in the earth's temperature which is caused by a build-up of carbon dioxide. This traps heat from the earth. The ice caps are melting, which causes sea levels to rise and low land to flood. The UK does not escape either. For example, East Anglia is at constant risk of flooding from the sea.

- Tropical areas like the Caribbean islands are experiencing extreme weather such as hurricanes, tornadoes and flooding. The UK has its share of freak weather. Many rivers had a red flood warning for the first time in 2000. Winters are getting warmer and weather is more unpredictable.

- Waste chemicals such as sulphur dioxide and nitrogen form clouds. These clouds drift from the UK to Scandinavia, where they release acid rain. Acid rain kills whole areas of forest and creates 'dead' lakes.

- Industrial waste affects rivers, wildlife, land, sea and air. The main problem is that this waste cannot be seen.

- Natural resources that took million of years to form – like oil and coal – are being used up.

- People are now eating fish from polluted seas. This causes allergies and illness.

Christians in action

People are starting to try to look after the world, although some action groups say 'too little, too late'. Voluntary agencies such as Christian Aid include green issues awareness in all their projects.

In parts of Eastern Europe, whole areas of forest are totally dead due to massive pollution. There is no money to pay for a clear-up.

Chernobyl 1986

In 1986, a nuclear power station in Chernobyl (Belarus) exploded. Even now, the land in that country is contaminated because of the explosion.

'Is our planet so small that we cannot share it with our sister and brother animals? Are our hearts so small there is no room for loving those whose world we share? Let us not forget, For all of us there is only one planet.'

YOU ARE THE FUTURE. DO YOU LIKE WHAT YOU SEE?

Be responsible. Actions have consequences.

LEARN from the PAST; LIVE in the PRESENT; PLAN for the FUTURE!!!

Slogans that demand a cleaner world.

Unfortunately, the people are so poor they are forced to eat local produce rather than 'cleaner' food from other countries. As a result babies born long after the explosion have birth defects. Many develop cancer such as leukaemia and thyroid cancer.

Christians on Merseyside bring children from Chernobyl to Liverpool to stay for a few weeks with local families. The children are given free eye tests, dental work and other medical help. Local companies give the children clothes, books and toys. Others are shown how to cope with their disabilities. A few weeks in clean air and eating good food can increase the children's lifespans.

Activities

1 Read the slogans on this page.
   a What does each slogan mean to you?
   b Design a suitable poster for one of the slogans. **C 2.3, IT 2.3, PS 1.1**

2 Make a list of local areas that you know are polluted. What is the problem with them? If you plot them on a map, is there a pattern? **IT 1.2, C 2.2, C2.1b**

Key points

- There are many forms of pollution. Some cannot be seen, but their effects on health and the environment *can* be seen.

- Pollution in one place often travels to another in the air or in water.

- It is not easy to put right the effects of pollution.

What can we do about the world?

Key terms

Habitat The natural home of an animal, plant or bird.

Attitudes

Most people would agree that the world is in a mess! Yet when it comes to doing something about it, there are some wonderful excuses.

- 'It has got nothing to do with me.'
- 'I blame the Council.'
- 'I blame the government.'
- 'I didn't make the mess, so why should I clear it up?'
- 'Industry did it, so they can clear it up.'
- 'God made the world, so he can look after it.'

Getting something done!

There are individuals, groups and governments, some of them Christians, who will do something about the world we live in. A teacher wrote this saying for her class.

> One drop of water in the sea cannot be seen;
> Put the drops together and you get an ocean!

This tells us that what one person does may seem very small, but joined together with other people's efforts it will achieve a great deal.

What can individuals do?

- They can write to their local council, MP or Prime Minister about green issues.

- They can organize groups to write letters or send e-mails.
- They can join groups such as Greenpeace, WWF or A Rocha (see page 7). These large groups have the power to change things.
- They can join local groups to keep their local area tidy, or help park rangers with their work.
- They can raise money for green issues – for example, by working in a charity shop.
- They can show they care by recycling – for example, taking bottles to the bottle bank or by making a compost heap in the garden.

What can groups do?

The National Trust is an example of a group that people can join. It looks after stately homes. It also owns a lot of coastal land and forests. It runs holidays where people (often teenagers) can do conservation work such as clearing ponds, building fences or mending footpaths.

Learn to recycle – everything can be used again.

Environmental groups can often put pressure on those they think are damaging our world.

Governments acting together can help the world to end pollution.

Greenpeace is an international group. It aims to make the world aware of green issues, sometimes in a dramatic way. For example, some of its members sprayed baby seals with harmless coloured dye so the seals would not be killed for their coats.

WWF is another international group. It aims to protect wildlife and their **habitats**. For example, WWF tries to stop elephants being killed for their ivory tusks.

What can a nation do?

- If people object to something, they should try to persuade their government to act. Governments will respond if it is a vote winner.

- People can ask the government to discuss green issues with other countries. For example, ministers raise conservation issues when they visit African nations. Or they might talk to the Russian Prime Minister about rusting Russian nuclear submarines that leak waste into the sea.

- Governments can meet to agree targets to reduce pollution. For example, in 1987 the **Montreal protocol** managed to ban CFCs. This could lead to the hole in the **ozone layer** closing in about 45 years from now.

Activities

a Find out about the work of a local group (for example, the Groundwork Trust) or a national group (for example, Greenpeace or WWF) by visiting www.heinemann.co.uk/hotlinks and clicking on this section.

b See if there are any projects near your school or where you live. Your local council should be able to help you with information.

c When you have found some information, give a short talk to your class (on your own or in pairs).

IT 2.1, 2.2, C 2.1b

Key points

- Conservation is possible! People are willing to help.

- Individuals can do something, even if only a little.

- Groups can do a lot to help and to raise awareness.

- Governments can pass laws to protect the environment.

Here you will find the relevant Bible passages you will need for the environment section. The set passage is written out. Then there is an explanation of what it means.

Set passage

(Creation) Genesis 1: 1–2: 3 (adapted)

In the beginning God created the heavens and the earth. Now the earth was formless and empty, darkness was over the surface of the deep, and the Spirit of God was hovering over the waters. And God said:

Day 1 'Let there be light.' He separated the light from darkness and called the light 'day' and the darkness 'night'.

Day 2 'Let there be an expanse between the waters to separate water from water.' God called the expanse 'sky'.

Day 3 'Let the water under the sky come together in one place, and let that dry land appear.' God called the dry land 'earth' and the waters 'sea'. 'Let the land produce vegetation, seed-bearing plants and trees that bear fruit.'

Day 4 'Let there be lights in the expanse of the sky to separate day from night, and let them serve as signs to mark seasons, days and years.' God created the sun, moon and stars.

Day 5 'Let the water teem with living creatures, and let birds fly above the earth.' God created the great creatures of the sea, all kinds of creatures that live in water and all kinds of birds. God told creatures to reproduce and increase in number.

Day 6 'Let the land produce living creatures, domestic and wild, large and small. Let us make man in our own image, in our likeness, and let them rule over the fish of the sea and the birds of the air, over the livestock, over all the earth, and over all the creatures that move along the ground.' Then God made human beings to be like him. He created them male and female, blessed them and said, 'Have many children, so your descendants will live all over the earth and bring it under their control. I am putting you in charge of the fish, birds and wild animals. I have provided all kinds of grain and fruits for you to eat. For the wild animals and birds I have provided leafy plants and grass for food.'

Day 7 The whole universe was completed. God had finished what he had been doing and stopped working. He blessed the seventh day and set it apart as a special day; because on that day he had completed his creation and stopped working.

And that is how the universe was created.

This passage has been discussed on pages 2–3. It is the key passage for environment questions. It tells us the early beliefs about the world. It explains why the world was created and that God wants humans to look after the world.

Other relevant passages

Exodus 23: 10–11

> For six years you are to sow your fields and harvest the crops, but during the seventh year let the land lie unploughed and unused. Then the poor among your people may get food from it, and the wild animals may eat what they leave. Do the same with your vineyard and your olive grove.

This explains how a field should be left fallow (not used) for one whole year out of every seven. The soil can then recover its goodness. Animals can eat plants that grow. Poor people can gather crops that grow naturally from self-seeding.

Today, organic farmers also use the idea of a fallow year. Christian groups take the idea to **developing countries**. There, farmers allow animal grazing for natural manure.

Psalm 19: 1–6

> The heavens declare the glory of God;
> the skies proclaim the work of his hands.
> Day after day they pour forth speech;
> night after night they display knowledge.
> There is no speech or language where their voice is not heard.
> Their voice goes out to all the earth;
> their words to the ends of the world.
>
> In the heavens [God] has pitched a tent for the sun,
> which is like a bridegroom coming forth from his pavilion,
> like a champion rejoicing to run his course.
> It rises at one end of the heavens and makes its circuit to the other;
> nothing is hidden from its heat.

The psalmist knows that God created the world. The whole world praises God. In those days, people believed that the sun moved across the sky. That is why the psalm describes it like a running track.

Leviticus 27: 30, 33

> A tithe of everything from the land, whether grain from the soil or fruit from the trees, belongs to the Lord; it is holy to the Lord.
>
> He must not pick out the good from the bad or make any substitution.

A **tithe** is one-tenth of everything that a person owns or earns. Jews had to give one-tenth of everything to God. This passage reminds Jews that only the best is good enough for God. A farmer could not keep the best for himself. This reminds us today that we should thank God for providing for us.

Activities

1. Using the Internet or an atlas of the ancient world, find out how ancient civilizations regarded the world. (You can find a Jewish idea on page 3.) **IT 2.1**

2. What do you think of the idea of **tithing**? Give reasons for your answer. Use the library and Internet to try to find out more about the idea of tithing. **C 1.1, 1.2**

3. Do you think organic farming is better than using modern chemicals to improve crops? **C 1.1, 1.2**

Exam questions to practise

Below are some sample exam questions. There are some tips from examiners to help you score good marks for the first four questions.

1 According to Genesis chapter 1, what did God think of the world he had created? (1) *(NEAB 2000, A2)*

2 What did God tell the first humans to do, according to Genesis chapter 1? (3) *(NEAB 2000, A2)*

3 What does the word 'stewardship' mean when referring to God's world? (3) *(AQA 2003)*

4 'Christians should leave the world in good condition for future generations.' Do you agree? Give reasons for your answer showing you have considered more than one point of view. (5) *(NEAB 2000, A2)*

Now try question 5 on your own. Before you write your answer, spend some time thinking about your approach.

5 Look at the slogan below.

> **If you want to change the world, start by changing YOUR ATTITUDE.**

a Would Christians agree with the slogan? Give reasons for your answer showing you have thought about more than one point of view. (5)

b Explain why it is so important to look after the world now. Refer to Christianity in your answer. (4)

How to do well

1 This tests your knowledge of the set passage. If you do not know the passage you will lose marks. You can find the answer on page 2.

2 There are three marks here, so try to write three different things God said. Remember, this is about Genesis chapter 1. You can turn to page 12 for help with this question.

3 This is worth three marks. Your answer must be a 'dictionary' definition of the term. You can find this in the glossary. Write in proper sentences.

4 This is an evaluation question. To gain full marks, you must give more than one point of view.

- Give one view for *and* one against the quote.

- You must refer to Christianity in your answer. Is it just down to Christians, or should the whole human race help?

- You must cover the whole point of the question to get full marks. You need to stress the key point.

Decisions on life and living: abortion and voluntary euthanasia

This chapter covers important issues about life and living. It is about the beginning and ending of life. Christians hold very strong views on both issues. Others have the right to express a point of view, too.

This section includes:

- What is abortion?
- What the Churches say
- Views for and against abortion
- What is voluntary euthanasia?
- For and against voluntary euthanasia
- Alternatives
- Bible passages
- Exam questions to practise

What is abortion?

Abortion is one of the most touchy subjects in this book. You must listen to all points of view, even if you do not agree with them.

The law in the UK

Before 1967, abortion was illegal. A woman with money could go to a private clinic for an illegal abortion. Poor women went to 'back street' clinics, where unqualified people performed the abortion. Sometimes these people used knitting needles for the operation. There was no pain relief, and hygiene was poor. Often women bled heavily. Some even died because they were afraid to go to hospital.

David Steel, a Christian MP, worked hard to change the law to allow women and girls to have safe abortions. The Abortion Act was passed in 1967.

Abortion Act 1967 (revised 1990)

Abortion is legal if there is a risk:

- to the mother's life

- to the mother's mental or physical health

- that the baby has a severe birth defect, or is unlikely to live after birth

- of harm to other children in the family.

Two doctors have to agree that the mother can have an abortion. The time limit is 24 weeks from **conception**. The father has no right to stop an abortion.

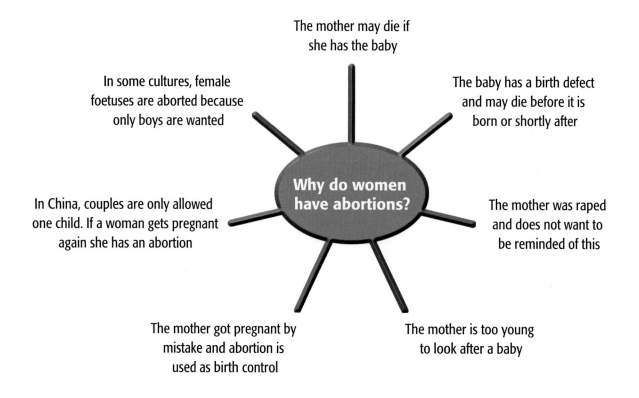

The mother may die if she has the baby

The baby has a birth defect and may die before it is born or shortly after

In some cultures, female foetuses are aborted because only boys are wanted

The mother was raped and does not want to be reminded of this

Why do women have abortions?

In China, couples are only allowed one child. If a woman gets pregnant again she has an abortion

The mother is too young to look after a baby

The mother got pregnant by mistake and abortion is used as birth control

Interview with Kathy

Hi! I'm Kathy. I'm fifteen, nearly sixteen. But I look a lot older. I first had sex when I was thirteen. It was with a Year 12 lad I met at a disco. We went out for six months, but then I felt tied down.

Then I met Pete. He was nineteen. We went out for six months. Sex was great and he was lovely. When I was ill and on antibiotics he looked after me. Even said we would get married. We weren't using condoms then, as I was on the pill.

Then horror! I was pregnant. Pete said he would stick by me, whatever.

I lost weight and was in pain and bleeding. They put me in hospital. I was on a drip and had scans and blood tests. Older, married mums 'tutted' at me. A doctor said things were bad and could get worse. She advised an abortion.

Pete went ballistic. He didn't want his child being killed. I said, 'You didn't use condoms.' He said, 'You were on the pill.' He stormed out. I was in a state. A woman chaplain came to see me. She talked about my options: school, ambitions to be a beautician and have my own salon, child care, my own health. Then we talked about fostering, adoption, keeping the baby with my mum helping.

I did have an abortion at twelve weeks – my decision. Pete came to see me … wants to start again. Well, we will see.

When does life begin?

There are different views about when life begins.

- Life begins at the moment of conception. To end the pregnancy means to kill a human being.

- Life does not begin until the baby can survive outside the mother's womb. It is part of the mother until it is born. The mother has the right to decide what to do with her own body.

- Life begins when the foetus has a heartbeat, or brain activity or a central nervous system (about 40 days old).

Activities

1 Do you think it is right that the father has no legal rights over a foetus? Should it be just the mother's decision? In groups, give reasons for your answers. **C 2.1a, WO 2.3**

2 Read the interview with Kathy (see opposite).
   a Do you think she was right to have an abortion? Give reasons
   b Do you think she should go back to Pete? Give reasons. **PS 2.1, C 2.1a**

Key points

- Abortion is a sensitive issue.

- In the UK, the 1967 Abortion Act made it legal to have an abortion.

- The most important question is 'When does life begin?'

What the Churches say

The Roman Catholic view

The Roman **Catholic** Church teaches that abortion is murder. Life begins at conception. In 1968, Pope Paul VI wrote a document called *Humanae Vitae*. The document said that for Roman Catholics abortion was wrong.

The Church of England view

In 1983, the **General Synod** (government) of the Anglican Church put out a statement. It said that the Church of England generally opposes abortion. However, there may be some reasons why it is better to have an abortion than to continue a pregnancy.

The Synod continued that 'the foetus is God-given life'. People should help and support mothers, and recognize their feelings and wishes. The statement goes on:

> 'The foetus has the right to live … as a member of a human family. Abortion … is a great moral evil.'

It advised that abortions should be carried out early in pregnancy.

In the 1997 and 2001 general elections, the General Synod advised its members to ask candidates about their views on abortion.

The views of other groups

Here are some other views about abortion.

- *Christians for Free Choice* say women should learn about their options and then ask God to guide them. It says you cannot make rules, as all cases are different.

- *SPUC* (Society for the Protection of the Unborn Child) aims to protect the life of the foetus from the time of conception. It is a **pro-life** society. It is not religious, but most of its members in the UK are Christians.

- *Marie Stopes International* says that all people have the human right to 'have a child by choice, not chance'. Marie Stopes International works in over 30 countries. It gives birth control advice and helps as well as cares for pregnant women.

- *BPAS* (British Pregnancy Advisory Service) gives good quality advice and services for women who wish to avoid pregnancy. It will carry out sterilization, vasectomy and crisis counselling. It is a **pro-choice** group.

The foetus at 28 weeks.

Interview with Thomas

My name is Thomas, known as Tom to my friends! I was born with spina bifida, which was quite severe. My mum found out when she had a scan. The doctors told her to have an abortion. Mum, being mum, went home to talk with dad then off to the vicar. The vicar's first question was whether they knew anything about spina bifida. As they didn't, he took them to a special school. There mum and dad talked to teachers and met kids with spina bifida.

Mum did keep me. When I was twelve I was able to go to the local secondary school with my helper. All my form helped me.

I'm sixteen now, got my GCSEs and am doing A levels – mainly because my girlfriend Ali is in the sixth form, too! If mum had had an abortion what a wasted life – and Ali would never have been lucky enough to meet me!

Activities

Find out more about:
a abortion
b methods of abortion at different weeks of pregnancy
c the risks involved.

A good place to start your research is the Society for the Protection of Unborn Children (SPUC) website at www.heinemann.co.uk/hotlinks. **IT 2.1, 2.3**

Key points

- People tend to be either for or against abortion.

- Christians are divided on the issue. Some of them hold extreme views.

- Some **denominations** want MPs to state their views on abortion at general elections.

Views for and against abortion

There are many arguments both for and against abortion. People will be able to justify their reasons and you must accept their views as being just as valid as yours.

Arguments for the right to choose

- Every woman has the right to choose, so long as she has information on all the options.

- Some Christians say that every child should be wanted. No woman should be forced to carry a child that is not wanted.

- The world population is growing. All couples should have the means to prevent pregnancy so that they can feed their other children.

- In the case of rape, many Christians would accept abortion. They realize that every time the mother looked at her baby, she would remember the horror of it all. The mother might fear the child would grow up to be violent.

- A woman might consider abortion if she had a life-threatening illness. The woman may already have other children at home. Should they lose their mum?

- Some would question the need to bring a disabled baby into the world, especially now there are tests that can determine early on if a child will be disabled. The mother has a choice.

- Many women see it as their **fundamental** right to choose an abortion.

Some would argue that a pregnant mother should be able to make her own choices about her baby.

Arguments against abortion

- Many Christians would say that abortion goes against the commandment 'Do not kill'. They believe that the foetus is a new life, so removing it is murder.

- Christians believe that God gives life and only he can take it away.

- Many Christians believe that a child is a gift from God. When you make love you should not exclude the possibility of conceiving. So if you do not want a baby, you should not have sex, or you should use a natural way of seeing if the woman is in her fertile time.

- The foetus has rights too, but it cannot voice its opinion.

- There is currently a lot of research about how much pain a foetus can feel. Some doctors claim the foetus is in agony as it dies.

- Many women suffer post-abortion **traumatic** stress. Some women will have guilty feelings more than 40 years later.

Interview with Jessica

I am pro-choice. I believe that:

- abortion carries less risk than pregnancy and childbirth

- every child should be wanted; abortion may prevent abuse

- nobody has the right to make me share their moral views

- Jesus never taught about abortion

- abortion must stay legal, in particular for incest and rape pregnancies

- if abortion is made illegal, back street clinics will open again.

Interview with Jane

I am pro-life. I believe that:

- an unborn foetus is a human being with basic human rights

- violence outside abortion clinics is wrong, but I see why they do it

- rape and incest are horrific **crimes** which are dealt with in courts of law, but that the unborn child has done no harm

- the **NHS** wastes resources on abortions

- the father should have rights too; this might make some men take a more responsible attitude towards family planning

- killing a foetus is murder, and the Bible says 'You shall not murder' (Exodus 20: 13).

Some people would say there is no argument strong enough to justify abortion.

Activities

1 In 1997, there was a general election in Britain. Candidates were often asked their views on abortion, before questions about issues such as education and the health service. Do you think this was right? In groups make a list of reasons for and against this. **C 1.1, 2.1a**

2 In pairs, on your own or in groups, write your own 'I am pro-choice' and 'I am pro-life' arguments. You could do this for a display. **C 1.3**

Key points

- Abortion is controversial.

- Some Christians will never accept abortion because they believe it is murder.

- Others would say you have to take each case alone, as each is unique.

- Some would try to show **compassion** – as Jesus did – and also be concerned about the quality of life of all involved.

What is voluntary euthanasia?

Voluntary euthanasia is a hot issue with Christians on both sides of the argument. The patient – and no one else – makes the decision. The patient may ask someone, often a doctor or relative, to help him or her to die. The person must be able to make a clear decision. If the relatives make the decision for the patient or the patient is in a coma, then this is not voluntary euthanasia.

Other names for voluntary euthanasia

Voluntary euthanasia has many names including **assisted suicide**, **mercy killing** and gentle, easy death.

- *Assisted suicide* is when someone helps a patient to die. Supporters of voluntary euthanasia do not agree that this is **suicide**. The law in the UK does not allow this. A person who helps someone to die may be charged with 'assisting a suicide'.

- *Mercy killing* also means bringing about a patient's death to avoid more pain or suffering. It is showing love (mercy). The patient may be unable to do this for him or herself. It can be compared to putting sick animals to sleep. In law, anyone who kills another person may be charged with murder.

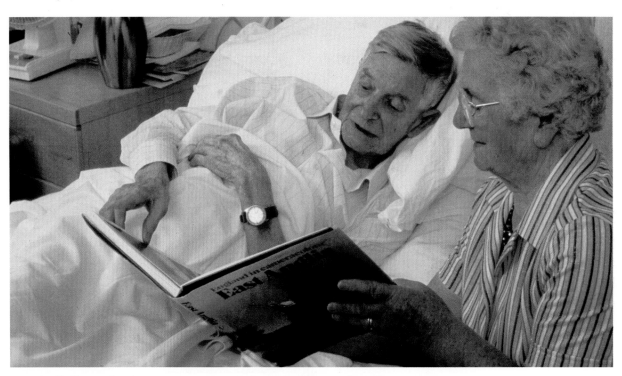

Terminally ill people often want peace and dignity in the way they die.

- *Gentle, easy death* – the patient wants to die quickly with **dignity** and in peace, maybe with family by their side.

Members of Exit can apply for a book on methods of dying. In the Netherlands, patients have the right to ask a doctor to be allowed to die, and their request will be considered.

Living will

When a patient does not wish to be kept alive by a machine, he or she can declare this in advance in a **living will**.

What Churches say

Different Churches give different advice on the subject of **euthanasia**. Different Christians have their own beliefs too.

- *Quaker* guidance states, 'We do not set down rules. We offer a process for working out the decision that is right for each individual person.'

- *Roman Catholic* guidance states euthanasia is wrong. Life is sacred. Only God can make decisions about death.

- *Church of England* says the rights of humans are valued. In 1993, the Synod published a report that said no change in the law was needed. In other words, a person has a right to refuse treatment but he (or she) does not have the right in law to die at a time of his choosing.

What other groups say

Exit wants a change in the law to allow greater flexibility concerning euthanasia. It also advises living wills so they are acceptable and legal in a court of law.

Exit: promoting euthanasia and advising on legal acceptability.

Activity

Why do you think voluntary euthanasia is still illegal in the UK? Discuss as a whole class or in groups (groups need to share their ideas). Visiting the Exit website at www.heinemann.co.uk/hotlinks might help you to make up your mind. **C 2.1a, IT 2.1**

Key points

- Voluntary euthanasia is when the patient decides he/she wants to die because he/she is going to die soon in any case, or is in great pain.

- Voluntary euthanasia is controversial.

- People on both sides watch events in the Netherlands carefully, where euthanasia is legalized, to see the effects on attitudes.

For and against voluntary euthanasia

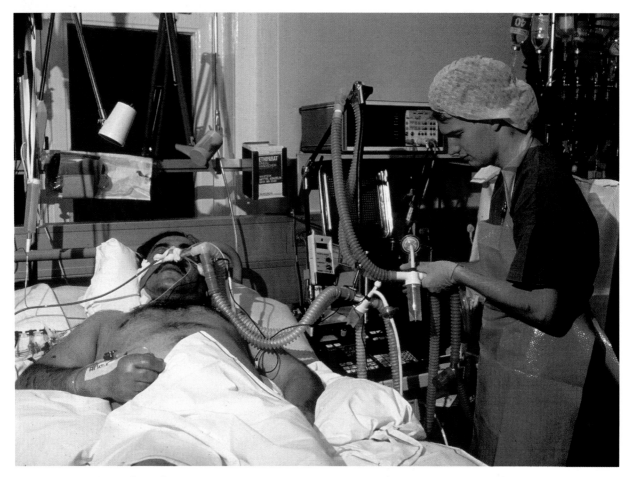

Should people have the right to request that they want to die?

There are arguments for and against voluntary euthanasia.

Arguments for voluntary euthanasia

- If a person has the right to eat or drink what he or she likes, smoke, pierce his or her body, then he or she should also have the right to decide when to die if his or her suffering gets too much.

- Some Christians believe that total healing will be in heaven, so all they are doing is speeding things up.

- Why should suffering be prolonged? Sometimes family and friends do not visit as they cannot cope with seeing their loved one in pain.

- The patient wants to die with dignity and believes he or she has that right. The patient may face loss of control over bodily functions. He or she fears having to have everything done for him or her.

- The patient wants to die in his or her own bed at home, with other family members there at the time of death.

- Some say that Jesus showed compassion and voluntary euthanasia is just that.

Arguments against voluntary euthanasia

- God gives life, so only he can decide when to take it away. Life is a precious gift. Voluntary euthanasia goes against the commandment 'Do not kill'.

- The patient might not be able to make a properly thought-out decision and might change his or her mind again on a good day.

- Doctors promise to save life. Voluntary euthanasia may be showing mercy, but it is not saving life.

- A miracle may take place or the treatment might work. Many Christians believe in miracles and they pray for healing.

- Christians believe that nursing the sick is one way of helping Jesus. He cured people of many illnesses.

- Some Christians believe that suffering is a way of strengthening faith and trust in God. They would say it is part of life and not for us to question.

Interview with Meg

I am Meg. And yes, I want to die! Does that shock you? I am 23 and I became **HIV positive** while in my teens – sharing beds with the lads at parties I guess. My dad took me home. I am in pain, unbearable at times, but I won't let the doctors pump me full of drugs. I'm into natural things – like using **Chinese herbs**. Dad pays for this. He is suffering too. He sees his daughter dying. I want to die before I have to have everything done for me – I mean everything, including the loo! I want to know when I will die. Each morning I wake up thinking 'Well, I am alive today.'

Meg has made it clear she does not want to be revived if her heart stops or be put on a life support machine. Neither does she want life-prolonging drugs. Her father supports her and her medical carers know.

Activities

1 Write a poem about voluntary euthanasia. (You may want to work in pairs.) It can be for or against, or it can put forward both views. When everyone has finished, all the poems can be read out loud to the class.
WO 2.2, 2.3

2 Reread the interview with Meg. Why does she wish to die now? Do you think she is right? Give reasons. **PS 2.1**

Key points

- The points for and against voluntary euthanasia can all be justified.

- One of the main arguments supporting it is that we should show compassion and respect the patient's wishes.

Alternatives

Key terms

Hospice A home for the care of the terminally ill.

People do have choices when they are dealing with life-and-death issues.

Alternatives to abortion

- If pregnancy would be a disaster, then use contraception properly. Girls should insist on their partner using a condom. Doctors say that in most cases of unwanted pregnancy, contraception has not failed, it has not been used!

- The baby can be given up for adoption.

- The baby can be fostered until the mother can cope.

- The woman can have her baby and seek help from **Social Services** and other groups. They offer practical help and home visits.

- Some women, especially young teenagers, go back to their own families, and all the relatives help look after the baby. Others go to live with the family of the father of the baby.

Alternatives to euthanasia

- Pain relief: many hospitals now have pain relief clinics with the latest ways of reducing pain.

- New painkillers: these are less addictive, have fewer side effects and are more efficient.

- **TENS machines** (first developed as pain relief in labour): these send pulses down the affected area and work on the nerves, allowing patients to move around.

- **Homeopathic** and herbal remedies (such as Chinese herbs).

- **Acupuncture**: this is very popular. It can help sickness and encourage well-being.

- Meditation, hypnotherapy or **yoga**: some people use these to ease their pain. They help relaxation.

- **Hospice**: this is a hospital for the terminally ill (see opposite). Hospices are run on a personal basis with experts to care for people.

There are many means of support for young mothers who feel they are not ready to cope with a young baby.

Hospices

Christian Knights (the Knights Templar) set up hospices to care for injured soldiers during the **Crusades**. In the Middle Ages, monks and nuns also set up hospitals to care for sick and dying people who could not pay for treatment. Monasteries had gardens where they grew herbs to make medicines.

In the twentieth century, a Christian doctor, Dame Cicely Saunders, worked to set up hospices. She said that we must change the attitude that 'we never talk about death'.

Hospices specialize in caring for people who are dying. (Hospitals are for people who hope to get well.) Specialist doctors help in pain management and the use of new medicines. Alternative therapies are available such as acupuncture, aromatherapy, relaxation and herbal treatments.

There are also many other staff – including nurses, physiotherapists, occupational health workers and counsellors. Chaplains from many churches visit patients. They are able to talk to patients and their families about death and what comes after.

Adults and children who are dying can go to a hospice for as long as is needed. They do not have to belong to a particular religion. There are, however, hospices set up by different religious groups. Here are two comments about hospices from interviews given at a local hospice.

> 'Anybody may come here regardless of religion, type of terminal illness, race, social class or ability to pay.'

> 'Hospices are charities built by the generosity of people who gave donations and grants, and funded by donations, grants and the continued generosity of supporters.'

Activities

Find out about one or more of these natural treatments:

a aromatherapy
b herbal treatments
c acupuncture
d yoga.

You might like to see if someone who has used some of these treatments can come to your school and talk about them. A local natural remedy clinic might send someone to do a demonstration and explain why these are thought to be good remedies. **C 2.2, IT 2.2**

Key points

- Opponents of abortion say there are many safe options instead of having an abortion, each having the welfare of baby and mother as the most important factor.

- Opponents of voluntary euthanasia point to the tremendous advances in pain relief and management of illnesses.

- The hospice movement aims to train more specialists in how to care for the dying.

Bible passages

Here you will find the relevant Bible passages that you will need for the abortion and voluntary euthanasia section. The set passages are written out. Then there is an explanation of what they mean.

Set passages

Exodus 20: 1–17
(Ten Commandments)

God spoke all these words:
'I am the Lord your God, who brought you out of Egypt, out of the land of slavery.

'You shall have no other gods before me.

'You shall not make for yourself an idol in the form of anything in heaven above or on the earth beneath or in the waters below. You shall not bow down to them or worship them; for I, the Lord your God, am a jealous God, punishing the children for the sin of the fathers to the third and fourth generation of those who hate me, but showing love to thousand generations of those who love me and keep my commandments.

'You shall not misuse the name of the Lord your God, for the Lord will not hold anyone guiltless who misuses his name.

'Remember the Sabbath day by keeping it holy. Six days you shall labour and do all your work, but the seventh is a Sabbath to the Lord your God. On it you shall not do any work, neither you, nor your son or daughter, nor your manservant or maidservant, nor your animals, nor the alien within your gates. For in six days the Lord made the heavens and the earth, the sea, and all that is in them, but he rested on the seventh day. Therefore the Lord blessed the Sabbath day and made it holy.

'Honour your father and your mother, so that you may live long in the land the Lord your God is giving you.

'You shall not murder.

'You shall not commit **adultery**.

'You shall not steal.

'You shall not give false testimony against your neighbour.

'You shall not covet your neighbour's house. You shall not covet your neighbour's wife, or his manservant or maidservant, his ox or donkey, or anything that belongs to your neighbour.'

The commandments deal with how you live your life in relationship to God, and with other people. Some Christians would use the commandment 'Do not kill' to support their view that abortion is wrong. It is murdering the unborn child. Many opponents of voluntary euthanasia would use it to support their argument that euthanasia is wrong.

1 Corinthians 6: 18–20
(Body as a temple)

Flee from sexual immorality. All other **sins** a man commits are outside his body, but he who sins sexually sins against his own body. Do you not know that your body is a temple of the **Holy Spirit**, who is in you, whom you have received from God? You are not your own; you were bought at a price. Therefore honour God with your body.

Paul says that God lives in our bodies as the Holy Spirit. So we should be careful what we do with our bodies in every aspect of our lives – including abortion and euthanasia.

Genesis 1: 26–27 (Creation)

Then God said, 'Let us make man in our image, in our likeness, and let them rule over the fish of the sea and the birds of the air, over the livestock, over all the earth, and over all the creatures that move along the ground.'

So God created man
in his own image,
in the image of God
he created him;
male and female
he created them.

Humans are special. God made the world first for humans.

Other relevant passages

Jeremiah 1: 5

Before I formed you in the womb I knew you,
before you were born I set you apart;
I appointed you as a prophet to the nations.

God has mapped out our lives even before our conception. He has chosen what we will do. So it is not for us to end a new life, because God may have great plans for that person.

Psalm 139: 13–16

For you [God] created my inmost being;
you knit me together in my mother's womb …
My frame was not hidden from you when I was made in the secret place.
When I was woven together in the depths of the earth,
your eyes saw my unformed body.
All the days ordained for me were written in your book before one of them came to be.

This says that God maps out our lives. That means *he* has decided when we will die, not us. God created the world and continues to create. Each new human is wonderfully made. God has worked out our role in life, so we should not prematurely end any life.

Luke 12: 4–7

[Jesus said] do not be afraid of those who kill the body and after that can do no more. But I will show you whom you should fear: Fear him who, after the killing of the body, has power to throw you into hell. Yes, I tell you, fear him. Are not five sparrows sold for two pennies? Yet not one of them is forgotten by God. Indeed, the very hairs of your head are all numbered. Don't be afraid; you are worth more than many sparrows.

God cares for us. We should respect God, who will judge our lives. If he cares for sparrows, then surely he treats humans as more precious.

Activities

1   Outline a Bible passage that Christians could use to support the idea that abortion (or voluntary euthanasia) is wrong. **C 2.2**

2   Try to explain the link between abortion (or euthanasia) and the Bible passages. **C 2.2**

Exam questions to practise

Below are some sample exam questions for paper 2A. To help you score full marks, the first two questions are followed by some tips from examiners.

1   **a**   Explain the term 'abortion'. (2)
    b   State two options a Christian might choose instead of having an abortion. (2)
            (NEAB 2000)

2   **a**   Explain the term 'voluntary euthanasia'. (2)
    b   Explain one reason why many Christians are against voluntary euthanasia. (2) *(NEAB 2000)*

Now try questions 3 and 4 on your own. Before you write your answers, spend some time thinking about your approach.

3   Explain a Bible passage that a Christian might use to support his or her belief that voluntary euthanasia is wrong. (4) *(based on AQA 2003)*

4   'Abortion can be right in some circumstances.' Do you agree? Give reasons for your answer showing you have thought about more than one point of view. Refer to Christianity in your answer. (5)

How to do well

1   **a**   Give a definition. Use the glossary at the end of this book to help you.
    b   Give two different options. Do not write about kinds of contraception. This question is about abortion, not contraception. Remember that a Christian response is needed.

2   **a**   Again, this is a definition. Make it clear who is choosing to die, and why.
    b   A Christian response is needed, but you do not need to use a Bible passage. Only a short answer is needed to fit the amount of space given. You could use one of the passages on pages 28–29. Which one do you know best?

Decisions on life and living: marriage and relationships

This section looks at Christian marriage. Churches have different opinions about issues such as remarriage in church. We look at the marriage vows. We ask how each vow affects the day-to-day life of each couple. Relationships can go wrong for many reasons. We think about attitudes to divorce and annulment. Finally, we study same-sex marriages and sex before marriage.

This section includes:

- Why get married?
- The wedding ceremony
- An Orthodox wedding ceremony
- Teaching about marriage
- When things go wrong
- Churches' attitudes to divorce and remarriage
- Sex before marriage
- Other relationships
- Bible passages 1
- Bible passages 2
- Exam questions to practise

Why get married?

Key terms

Wedding The marriage service.

Marriage Being married.

Vows Solemn promises in the wedding ceremony between husband and wife.

Marriage: fairytale or reality?

The fairy tale and the reality

Getting married! Some magazines say it is a girl's dream: engagement ring, fairy tale **wedding**, expensive dress, gifts, honeymoon, hunk of a husband. For the man it could mean a gorgeous wife who he can show off, and who will take care of all his needs. Happy ever after?

In 1981 this scenario was played out for real: Prince Charles and Lady Diana got married. Millions watched. Yet it was no fairy tale. Things went wrong and eventually they got divorced. But, despite a high **divorce** rate, people continue to marry.

A Christian marriage

The Church of England 2000 *Book of Common Worship* wedding service sums up the Christian purpose of **marriage** (see below). A Christian wedding takes place with God as a witness.

Christian purpose of marriage

In the presence of God, Father, Son and Holy Spirit.

We have come together to witness the marriage of [name] and [name].

To pray for God's blessing on them, to share their joy and celebrate love.

Marriage is the gift of God in creation.

The couple shall be united with one another, heart, body and mind.

The gift of marriage brings husband and wife together in the delight and tenderness of sexual union and joyful commitment to the end of their lives.

It is given as the foundation of family life in which children are [born and] **nurtured**, in good times and bad.

Marriage is a way of life made holy by God.

Marriage is a sign of unity and loyalty.

No one should enter into it lightly or selfishly, but reverently and responsibly in the sight of almighty God.

[Name] and [name] are now to enter this way of life; they will give their consent to the other and make solemn **vows**. In token of this they will give and receive rings.

Marriage is the right relationship for making love. It is a sign of commitment; it is the relationship into which children are born and cared for. In good times and difficult times families support each other. Getting married is a serious matter; there are important vows to take.

Can you marry anyone?

In the UK if you are already married, you cannot marry again until divorced or the death of your **spouse**. There are also certain other rules.

Who cannot get married

Marriage between a person and any of the following relatives is illegal:

- parent
- child
- adopted child
- grandparent
- grandchild
- sibling (brother or sister)
- aunt or uncle
- niece or nephew.

What are the rules about weddings?

The Church of England says that weddings must take place between 8 am and 6 pm.

In the Church of England, one of the couple must have lived in the parish where the wedding will take place for at least fifteen days. **Banns** must be read out in each of the parishes of the couple for three weeks before the wedding. The Banns say who the couple are and their 'marital status' – for example, 'bachelor'. This gives the congregation a chance to say why the couple may not marry in law.

Are mixed marriages a problem?

A mixed marriage is when a husband and wife belong to different religions or racial groups – for example, Christian/Muslim or white/Asian. Many mixed marriages work well, but some face problems. For example, a Christian/Muslim couple might face these difficulties.

- Where will they get married? A mosque or a church? Or will they have a **civil wedding**?

- If they have children, which religion will they follow? Will the children be given Muslim or Christian names?

Activities

1 Look at the Christian purposes of marriage on page 32. Working in pairs, write down what you think is the most important reason for marriage. Why do you think this? **WO 1.1, C 2.1a**

2 **a** Think of one problem a mixed marriage couple might face.
   b Work out a solution, then think why it might/might not work. **C 1.1**

Key points

- Marriage is regarded as a serious life-long commitment.

- All Christian denominations regard marriage as the right background for sex and raising children.

- Problems can and do arise in mixed marriages. These problems are often about raising children.

The wedding ceremony

(Key terms)

Sacrament A religious ceremony or sign with inner meaning. Roman Catholics regard marriage as a sacrament.

Catechism Learning through questions and answers.

Order of service

The Order of Service below is from the Church of England. Most denominations will have a similar service.

If the couple are to take **Holy Communion** or the Nuptial **Mass**, this will usually take place before the Registration.

Marriage vows

One of the most important parts of the wedding service is when the couple take their vows. The key word to sum up the vows is 'commitment'.

There are eight vows that are usually made during the wedding ceremony. These vows are listed opposite.

Church of England Order of Service

Entry	The Bride, her father (or other relative) and attendants process to the front of the church. The bridegroom stands on her right.	**Exchange of rings**	The husband and wife exchange rings.
Hymn	Everyone sings.	**Announcement**	The couple are now husband and wife! The vicar reminds the people that nobody must break the bond of marriage. It has been made before God.
Welcome	The vicar welcomes those present and reads the Christian Purpose of Marriage.		
Declaration	The vicar asks the people if anyone knows of any reason in law why the couple cannot marry.	**Prayers and blessing**	Asking God to help and bless the couple throughout their marriage.
		Hymn(s)	Everyone sings.
Reading	From the Bible or other sources.	**Registration**	The couple sign the Register. Two other witnesses must sign, and so must the vicar.
Sermon	The vicar may give a talk.	**Final prayer**	Given by the vicar.
Vows	The couple make promises to each other.	**The couple leave**	The couple leave the church, followed by their friends and family.

Vows made during the wedding ceremony

1 I [name], take you [name], to be my husband/wife.

2 To have and to hold from this day forward.

3 For better, for worse.

4 For richer, for poorer.

5 In sickness and in health.

6 To love and to cherish.

7 Till death us do part.

8 According to God's holy law, and in the presence of God I make this vow.

from *The Book of Common Worship*, 2000.

The main theme of the marriage vows is commitment to each other. Here are the meanings of the vows.

1 The marriage is legal in the law of your country. 'I take you …' means that the person agrees to marry this person and is not being forced into marriage.

2 The couple are together as from today.

3 The couple will stay together in bad times as well as good times.

4 When money is tight, they will not split up just because they cannot buy what they please.

5 It is good if both partners are well. But if one is ill, then it is important to 'be there' for the sick one and take care of one another. This can bring the couple closer together.

6 The partners agree to love each other, take care of each other, and respect each other.

7 Marriage is for life.

8 This is based on God's Law in the Bible. These are serious vows.

Marriage is a sacrament

Roman Catholics and many other Christians believe that marriage is a **sacrament**. They believe strongly in life-long marriage. Others may say that the vows are 'declarations of intent'. People mean to keep them, but you have to allow for situations where the vows cannot be kept any more.

Catechism

In 1985, the **Catechism** said:

> Marriage is the sacrament in which baptized men and women vow to belong to each other in a permanent and exclusive sexual partnership of loving mutual care, concern and shared responsibility, in the hope of having children and bringing up a family.

Printed by the Catholic Truth Society.

Activities

1 Make up a set of vows that you would have at your wedding. Explain why you have chosen these vows. C 1.3, WO 2.2

2 Do you agree that a couple should be able to marry anywhere, such as in castles or on a beach? Give reasons. C 2.1a

Key points

- There are similar key parts in the Christian service in all churches.

- The most important part is sharing the vows, which are similar in all churches.

- The vows are serious, made in front of God.

An Orthodox wedding ceremony

The Orthodox wedding ceremony is different from weddings in other Christian churches. The symbolic acts are more important than the spoken word. An Order of Service is set out below.

Betrothal

The **betrothal** takes place at the doors of the church. The couple promise to love each other and be faithful. They exchange rings that have been blessed as a sign of this love and faithfulness. They hold lit candles as a sign that God is present. The people sing a special hymn.

The Gospel Book

This contains the four **Gospels**. It may be richly decorated and very old. It rests on the Holy Table. The priest sings 'The Three Great Prayers of Marriage', which make four points:

- God made human beings to rule over Creation
- the couple should have children
- they should care for the world
- their marriage is a sign of the unity between Christ and his church.

Coronation (crowning)

The priest places crowns over the heads of the bride and groom. The crowns may be made of gold and silver, or leaves and flowers. This depends on where the church is located.

The crowning means the couple are now married. It also means they are king and queen for the day.

The couple make their promises to each other.

The couple are crowned by the priest; they are king and queen for the day.

Bible readings and prayer

Two passages are read:

- 1 Corinthians 13 – all about love.

- John 2, about the wedding at Cana.

The priest leads the couple and the congregation in short prayers. This is followed by the Lord's Prayer.

Bible readings are an integral part of the Orthodox service.

Cup of wine

The couple take three sips of wine from the same cup. This is a sign that they now share a life together. It also is a symbol for the Trinity. While the people sing a hymn, the priest leads the couple round the Holy Table three times. This is a sign that marriage is eternal, with no beginning and no end.

The couple share wine from the same cup to symbolize the common life they will share now they are married.

Activities

1   How does the Orthodox wedding ceremony differ from other denominations? **C 1.1, 1.2**

2   Get into groups of no more than six. Using a large piece of paper, make a list of what is the same and what is different. Any surprises? **WO 2.1, 2.2**

Key points

- An Orthodox wedding is very different from other Churches.

- It focuses on symbolic actions rather than words.

- The most important part is the crowning. The couple are king and queen of a new part of God's kingdom here on earth.

Teaching about marriage

Here we will look at marriage as a sacrament and some different types of love.

Sacraments

Sacraments are ceremonies that are symbols with an inner meaning. Most Protestant Churches (such as Methodist) believe only **Baptism** and Holy Communion are sacraments. These are the ones that Jesus began. Other Churches, such as Roman Catholic, Anglican and Orthodox, accept up to five additional sacraments:

- confirmation
- Holy Communion/Mass
- marriage
- ordination
- anointing the sick and dying.

Marriage as a sacrament

For those who believe marriage is a sacrament, God is their witness every day. The symbolic actions in the wedding point to this. They believe the relationship between husband and wife includes God. God will help them to make a good marriage.

Controversy

In St Paul's letter to the Ephesians, he said: 'Wives obey your husbands' (see page 48 for the full text). In old wedding services, wives had to promise to obey their husbands. This could mean a woman had no say regarding their sex life, for example. A husband could also take all his wife's money and property. In any case, what about the husband's duty in marriage?

This sentence was written nearly 2000 years ago, when wives became the property of their husbands upon marriage. Also, it has been taken out of context.

Yes, sir!

Paul also said, 'Husbands, love your wives. Husbands ought to love their wives as their own bodies.' That was revolutionary in his day.

What did Paul mean?

A wife had to obey her husband, but the husband must respect his wife's wishes and not force her to do anything against her will.

In the ancient world, men and women had separate roles. Mainly, men had jobs, got the best price for things and entertained visitors. Woman had children and brought them up. They ran the household, and saw to the housework and cooking. It was important that husband and wife worked together.

Types of love

The word 'love' in English can have many meanings. It can mean 'I love fish and chips' or 'I love my granny' or 'I love my husband/wife'. The Greek language has many words for love. Some of them are shown opposite.

- *Philos* – the love that people have for friends. Sometimes called platonic or 'brotherly love'. It is not a sexual love, but deep friendship.

- *Eros* – romantic or sexual love. It grows from attraction and desire for another person.

- *Agape* (pronounced 'a-ga-pay') – Christian love. The kind of love that results in taking care of people in need. St Paul said this was the highest and purest form of love.

- *Storge* – love for family members. The love of parents for their children, and children for their parents. The love between brothers and sisters.

- *Love of things* – really means 'like', or even 'like a lot'.

Activities

1 List any couples you know who have been married for 25, 30, 40, 50 or more years. (These may be grandparents, other relatives or famous people.) Try to find out the secret of their successful marriages.
PS 2.1

2 Reread the text on different types of love.
   a In groups, list examples of each type of love.
   b Do you think people use the word 'love' too much? Give reasons.
   C 2.1a

Key points

- Christians believe that marriage is more than just a set of vows. It is making promises in front of God.

- The words of Paul about marriage in Ephesians were written for society 2000 years ago, but can be relevant in the twenty-first century.

- Some women still choose to promise to obey their husbands in the marriage vows.

When things go wrong

Key terms

Adultery When a married person has sex by consent with a person other than their partner (spouse). It is sometimes called 'having an affair' or 'extra-marital sex'.

Divorce The legal ending of a marriage. The couple can marry other people.

Marriages do not always last forever.

Before the twentieth century divorce was rare. A woman who was divorced usually lost everything and there was rarely a divorce settlement. However, over the last 100 years there have been gradual reforms in the law.

Law reform in marriage

- *1971 (Divorce Reform Act):* now a divorce could be given for **adultery**, cruelty or being separated for more than two years.

- *1984:* the 1971 act was updated. Only one year of separation was needed, not two.

- *1995 (discussion paper):* it was suggested that couples ought to have counselling before asking for divorce. The idea of proving the fault of the other was removed.

- *1998:* more guidelines to help those just married or engaged such as videos giving advice on several issues like mortgages, banks and making a will.

When Christians might accept divorce

- Where there is violence, many Christians agree that it is better for the abused partner and children to leave.

- Many Christians quote Matthew 5: 27–32 (see page 48); divorce is allowed for adultery.

Why couples get divorced

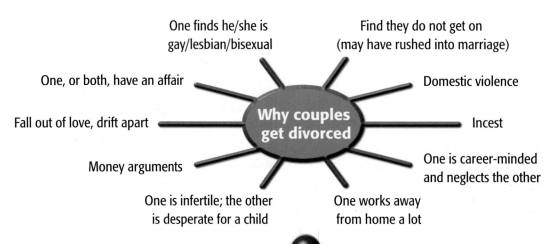

One finds he/she is gay/lesbian/bisexual

Find they do not get on (may have rushed into marriage)

One, or both, have an affair

Domestic violence

Fall out of love, drift apart

Why couples get divorced

Incest

Money arguments

One is career-minded and neglects the other

One is infertile; the other is desperate for a child

One works away from home a lot

- Some refer to 1 Corinthians 7 (see page 49). Paul said a Christian was not bound in marriage if his or her unbelieving partner walks out. Christians still believe this applies.

When Christians are against divorce

- Jesus said divorce was wrong (Mark 10, see page 50). He added to Malachi, who said God hates divorce.

- Christians believe marriage is for life. They make promises in front of God. If marriage is a sacrament, then only God can end it.

- People should be prepared to work at their marriages. If they work through the rough times, this will make their marriage stronger.

- People should get advice and help. They should think of the effect on their children. 'Quickie divorces' are not the answer.

Where couples can get advice

Marriage Care

Marriage Care (formerly the Catholic Marriage Advisory Council) wants to show compassion to couples in trouble. It recognizes the effects of divorce and separation on the whole family. It recognizes that only the couples themselves can save their marriages.

There are 73 Marriage Care centres. They work for the whole community, not just Roman Catholics. They run marriage preparation classes, too.

Relate

Relate is a non-religious organization, but many Christians use it or work for it. It has 2500 counsellors. It is independent and free from government control. Relate will help any adult or young person who is having relationship problems.

CARE (Christian Action Research and Education)

Many churches, especially **evangelical churches**, support this group. It writes teaching material and organizes courses such as 'Talking to your children' and 'Talking to your spouse'. It aims to show Jesus' compassion and supports family values.

Activities

1   Why do you think people have affairs? Make a list of reasons. **PS 2.1**

2   Act out the following role-play. You will need three people – the marriage counsellor (male or female), the wife and the husband.

   The couple are always arguing and criticizing each other. They do not go out together. The wife has headaches. The husband says he does not like his wife's clothes. The wife says she does not like his friends, and so on. The wife has 'dragged' her husband to see the counsellor. This is the first session.

   Act out the therapy sessions, which you can make serious or humorous. Practise and perform to the rest of the class. **C 2.1b, WO 2.3**

Key points

- Marriages are meant for life, but sadly some just do not work out.

- One key reason for divorce is abuse of the partner – domestic violence.

- Some Christians are against divorce on *any* grounds.

- There are many agencies that provide counselling.

Churches' attitudes to divorce and remarriage

Attitudes to divorce

Different churches have different opinions about divorce, but they all say marriage is meant for life.

- The Church of England does not approve of divorce. It teaches that marriage is for life. It says that when they make the vows, the couple should fully intend to keep them. However, it accepts that sometimes things change and the vows cannot be kept.

- The Roman Catholic Church does not accept divorce. It will offer **annulment** in special cases – for example, if one of the couple was forced into marriage, if the couple were unable to have sex, or if one of them was mentally ill. This is not a legal ending in the UK. The couple will still have to go to a divorce court.

- Some Free Churches believe that marriage ends when love ends, so divorce may be the desirable option.

In a Roman Catholic wedding, vows are made for life.

- The Orthodox Church says that on the wedding day every couple must fully mean to stay married. But in some cases the couple need to be set free from their vows.

Attitudes to remarriage

The question of whether a divorced person can get married again in church to a new person is hotly argued.

- The Church of England is divided. Since 2001 vicars are allowed to decide, with the guidance of their Bishop, whether to allow a **remarriage**. Different areas of the church made rules to decide the circumstances in which a person may remarry in church.

- The Roman Catholic Church will not allow the remarriage of divorced people and does not have a Service of Blessing. They say the vows were made for life and cannot be broken. If divorced people do remarry they are not allowed to take Holy Communion (Mass).

- The Methodist Church treats each request for remarriage in church as a separate case. Sometimes only regular churchgoers will be given a second chance and are married in church. The attitude is that we all make mistakes and need second chances.

- The Orthodox Church in some countries has the authority to give divorces as well as marry people (this is not allowed in the UK). The Orthodox teaching says people can remarry in church because God forgives past mistakes.

Quotes

The Roman Catholic Catechism states these things.

> Even if divorced people remarry legally they cannot take Communion; they disobey God's law. (Catechism 1650)

The remarried spouse commits adultery, as does his new wife. (Catechism 2384)

Divorce is a serious breaking of God's law. It breaks [the couple's] promises to live with each other until death. (Catechism 2384)

Divorce is wrong as it brings conflict into the family and the community. It causes children to be torn between mum and dad. (Catechism 2385)

Activities

1 Imagine you are a Roman Catholic or Church of England priest/vicar. A couple want to be married in your church, but one of them is divorced. They live in the parish and sometimes go to church. Working in pairs or small groups discuss the following questions.
   a How would you justify your refusal to marry them in church?
   b What advice would you give them?
   c What would the couples say in their defence? **C 2.1a, WO 2.3**

2 If you were allowed to marry the couple in church, would you? Give reasons. **PS 2.1, 2.3**

Key points

- All denominations teach that marriage is intended to be for life.

- The Roman Catholic Church does not allow remarriage after divorce.

- The Church of England does accept there may be situations where there will be divorce.

- There are churches that will remarry people.

Sex before marriage

The 1960s were seen by many as a period of sexual freedom.

People have always disagreed about sex before marriage. When the pill became available in the 1960s and 1970s, more people felt safe enough to chance one-night stands. The **AIDS** scare of the 1980s led more people to use condoms. This would prevent the spread of **disease**, as well as preventing pregnancy.

What the churches say

- Many Christians who attend the Church of England say vicars do not preach about sex before marriage, living together and relationships. Many young people are confused about what is right and wrong. They do not get a clear message from the Church of England. However, some churches do give clear teaching.

- The Roman Catholic Church has clear teaching even if many of its members do not agree with it. Sex before marriage is called **fornication**. Their teaching says, 'It is against God's law; [sex] is for married couples and the making of children.'

Living together

Living together is still a hot issue in the twenty-first century.

Is living together right …?

- You can make your own commitment to each other without the need for a marriage certificate.

- A wedding can be costly, especially if you have a white wedding, big reception and exotic honeymoon.

- A lot of people, including some Christians, say the divorce rate is high, so it might be better to have a trial marriage. They might say that if you bought an expensive car you would test-drive it first!

… or is living together wrong?

- In 1992, the Church of England sent out a report that said the Church recognizes that many people live together. However, it is concerned that couples will lose the support of a family.

- The Roman Catholic Church sees living together as the same as sex before marriage.

- It is easier to get out of the relationship, so there is no incentive to make the relationship work.

- Many of the older generations say if you get pregnant the mother will be an 'unmarried mother' and the child branded 'illegitimate'.

- Some people think living together is 'living in sin'. Christians say sex is more 'special' if you wait until marriage. There is always a chance of having a baby. Christians believe the best place to bring up a child is within marriage.

- Christians who regard marriage as a sacrament (see page 38) believe God is with them, binding them together. They believe that a man and woman belong to each other in a 'permanent, exclusive, sexual partnership'. This can only happen within marriage.

Should you wait to have sex?

Many teenagers have sex so that their friends will not laugh at them. They want to be just the same as others. This is called 'peer pressure'.

In the USA some teenagers got fed up with pressure to have sex, and with being seen as odd because they were still virgins at sixteen. They talked on the Internet and formed a group called 'True Love Waits'. Most of them were about twelve or thirteen years old. The local church had a ceremony: the teenagers signed a pledge card and received a ring as a sign of their promise to be sexually pure until they got married. Both girls and boys joined this group.

Some Christian care centre workers feel this is another kind of pressure. How can twelve year-olds know how they will feel about sex when they are older?

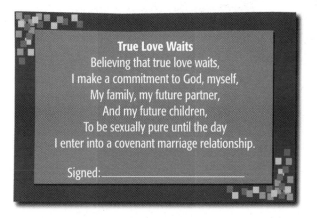

True Love Waits
Believing that true love waits,
I make a commitment to God, myself,
My family, my future partner,
And my future children,
To be sexually pure until the day
I enter into a covenant marriage relationship.

Signed:_____

Activities

1 Do you think people are making a fuss about nothing regarding living together? Discuss in groups of two or three. **C 2.1a, PS 2.1, WO 2.3**

2 Reread the passage entitled 'Should you wait to have sex?'. In groups answer the following questions.
   a Why did the teenagers form their group?
   b Are the pressures to have sex the same in the UK or different? Give reasons.
   c Why are some people concerned about True Love Waits? Are you? **C 1.1, 1.2, WO 1.2**

3 Is there a difference between **casual sex** before marriage, and living together? Give reasons for your answer. **C 2.1a, PS 2.1 WO 2.3**

Key points

- Many people cannot see the problem with couples living together.

- Some regard living together as practise for marriage. Other Christians say that living together spoils the specialness of marriage.

Other relationships

As well as marriage between a man and a woman, we will think about other types of relationship. We also need to think about **fidelity** (faithfulness), **chastity** (sexual purity) and **celibacy** (not having sex).

Sex or not?

- *Fidelity* is an old English word that means 'to be faithful'. It means you only have sex with your partner once married. Jesus taught that just by looking at another person in the wrong way you were sinning; especially as the thought may lead to action.

- *Chastity* is an old word that is still used today. A person decides to stay a virgin until his or her wedding night.

- *Celibacy* means a person decides not to marry or have sex. It can be forever, a long while or a short while. One reason might be to serve God better without having to worry about a family. Roman Catholic priests have to accept celibacy. People who become monks and nuns make the same vow.

Same-sex marriages

In the UK, at present same-sex marriages are forbidden. In countries such as the USA there are same-sex weddings, but they are only legal in Massachusetts which became the first state to grant marriage licenses to same-sex couples in May 2004.

Two people of the same sex decide to have a formal wedding service, but it is not legal.

Some Christians say that same-sex relationships are to blame for the spread of **HIV** and AIDS. They say **homosexual** relationships should not be tolerated.

Church of England view
The Church of England is divided on this issue with many opinions.

1987: a big row!
A report to the **General Synod** (council) said that sex belonged to marriage so this cannot apply to homosexual or lesbian sex.

And in 1991!
A 1991 report discussed Bible teaching, modern Christian thinking and church rules about same-sex relationships. The report said that Christians should not hate homosexual people and must protect them if they are treated badly.

Roman Catholic view
The Roman Catholic Church is very clear in its teaching: homosexual sex is wrong. They quote two Bible references – Leviticus 18: 22 and Romans 1: 26–27.

Family life
Christians place a high value on family life. There are two main types of family:

- nuclear family – parents and children
- extended family – parents, children, grandparents and other relatives who may live in the same house or in the same area.

The introduction to the Church of England wedding service stresses the importance of family life (see pages 32–33). Christian parents should:

- nurture their children – look after them from birth and take care of their needs

- teach them about their religion and about what is right and wrong.

The Bible supports this. For example in Exodus 20 one of the ten commandments is: 'Respect your father and mother.' Ephesians 6: 1–4 states 'Obey your parents.'

Christians think of the Church as a family. Christians may call each other 'brothers and sisters in Christ'. They call God 'our Father'. Jesus once said all his followers were brothers and sisters. The Church welcomes children into the family of the Church at their baptism. They will grow up as Christians and make their own commitment to their faith in the ceremony of Confirmation.

Activity
The following activity is best done in small groups due to the sensitive subject matter.

Should marriage be legal for homosexuals as long as they are over eighteen years old? Give reasons. **C 2.1a, WO 2.2, 2.3**

Key points
- There are types of relationships other than marriage which many in society will accept.
- The Church is divided, despite specific teaching, over the issue of homosexual relationships.

Here you will find the relevant Bible passages that you will need for the marriage and relationships section. The set passages are written out. Then there is an explanation of what they mean.

Set passages

Matthew 5: 27–32 (Adultery and divorce)

You have heard that it was said, 'Do not commit adultery.' But I tell you that anyone who looks at a woman lustfully has already committed adultery with her in his heart. If your right eye causes you to sin, gouge it out and throw it away. It is better for you to lose one part of your body than for your whole body to be thrown into hell. And if your right hand causes you to sin, cut it off and throw it away. It is better for you to lose one part of your body than for your whole body to go into hell.

It has been said, 'Anyone who divorces his wife must give her a certificate of divorce.' But I tell you that anyone who divorces his wife, except for her marital unfaithfulness, causes her to become an adulteress, and anyone who marries the divorced woman commits adultery.

Jesus answers a question about remarriage and divorce. He actually adds to the teaching and makes it harder. He makes it clear that divorce is wrong and the only reason for it could be adultery. He then goes on to what is regarded by some as harsh teaching.

1 Corinthians 6: 18–20 (The body as a temple)

Flee from sexual immorality. All other sins a man commits are outside his body, but he who sins sexually sins against his own body. Do you not know that your body is a temple of the Holy Spirit, who is in you, whom you have received from God? You are not your own; you were bought at a price. Therefore honour God with your body.

Paul reminds us to look after our bodies and be careful what we do with them. This is because God's Holy Spirit lives in our bodies.

Ephesians 5: 21–33 (Husbands and wives)

Wives, submit to your husbands as to the Lord. For the husband is the head of the wife as Christ is the head of the church, his body, of which he is the Saviour. Now as the church submits to Christ, so also wives should submit to their husbands in everything.

Husbands, love your wives, just as Christ loved the church and gave himself up for her to make her holy… In this same way, husbands ought to love their wives as their own bodies. He who loves his wife loves himself. After all, no one ever hated his own body, but he feeds and cares for it, just as Christ does the church – for we are members of his body. 'For this reason a man will leave his father and mother and be united to his wife, and the two will become one flesh.' Each one of you also must love his wife as he loves himself, and the wife must respect her husband.

No one should hate his or her own body. Instead he or she should feed it and take care of it, just as Christ does the church – for we are members of his body.

Other relevant passages

1 Corinthians 7: various verses

The husband should fulfil his marital duty to his wife, and likewise the wife to her husband. The wife's body does not belong to her alone but also to her husband. In the same way, the husband's body does not belong to him alone but also to his wife. (3–4)

Now to the unmarried and the widows I say: It is good for them to stay unmarried, as I am. But if they cannot control themselves, they should marry, for it is better to marry than to burn with passion.

To the married I give this command (not I, but the Lord): A wife must not separate from her husband. If she does, she must remain unmarried or else be reconciled to her husband. And a husband must not divorce his wife.

To the rest I say this (I, not the Lord): If any brother has a wife who is not a believer and she is willing to live with him, he must not divorce her. And if a woman has a husband who is not a believer and he is willing to live with her, she must not divorce him. (8–13)

But if the unbeliever leaves, let him do so. A believing man or woman is not bound in such circumstances. (15)

An unmarried man is concerned about the Lord's affairs – how he can please the Lord. But a married man is concerned about the affairs of this world – how he can please his wife – and his interests are divided. An unmarried woman or virgin is concerned about the Lord's affairs: Her aim is to be devoted to the Lord in both body and spirit. But a married woman is concerned about the affairs of this world – how she can please her husband. (32–34)

There are many points here, but remember Paul was writing for his time.

- The husband and wife belong to each other.

- Paul preferred the single life, but if you need sex then you should get married.

- If a husband or wife are married to an unbeliever, and the unbeliever cannot cope with a Christian spouse and walks out, then they can get divorced.

- If you want to serve God, it is better to be single so you can devote yourself to God. A married person has divided loyalties (may not know who to please).

Activities

1 Is it practical to expect couples to stay together in cases of adultery? Give reasons. **C 2.1a**

2 Explain in your own words why Paul's teaching about marriage in Ephesians 5 is so controversial. **C 2.2, PS 2.1**

Bible passages 2

Other relevant passages (cont.)

Proverbs 31: selection from verses 10–31

A wife of noble character who can find?
She is worth far more than rubies.
Her husband has full confidence in her
and lacks nothing of value.
She brings him good, not harm,
all the days of her life. (10–12)

She gets up while it is still dark;
she provides food for her family
and portions for her servant girls. (15)

She sees that her trading is profitable,
and her lamp does not go out at night. (18)

She opens her arms to the poor
and extends her hands to the needy. (20)

She makes coverings for her bed;
she is clothed in fine linen and purple.
Her husband is respected at the city gate,
where he takes his seat among the elders
of the land. (22–23)

She watches over the affairs of her
household
and does not eat the bread of idleness.
Her children arise and call her blessed;
her husband also, and he praises her:
'Many woman do noble things,
but you surpass them all!'
Charm is deceptive, and beauty is fleeting;
but a woman who fears the Lord is to be
praised.
Give her the reward she has earned,
and let her works bring her praise at the
city gate. (27–31)

This is the 'ideal' wife 3000 years ago. She is the one who looks after her family and the servants. She is also running a business, so she works long hours. Her husband is one of the respected elders. In the days of this description, the elders of a city used to sit at the main gate to dispense free justice and advice. She, too, is obviously respected. The family is rich. She is dressed in purple, the most expensive dye. But she considers the poor and needy. All her family love her. What could we learn from this?

Mark 10: 2–12

Some Pharisees came and tested [Jesus] by asking: 'Is it lawful for a man to divorce his wife?'

'What did Moses command you?' he replied.

They said, 'Moses permitted a man to write a certificate of divorce and send her away.'

'It was because your hearts were hard that Moses wrote you this law,' Jesus replied, 'But at the beginning of creation God "made them male and female". "For this reason a man will leave his father and mother and be united to his wife, and the two will become one flesh." So they are no longer two, but one. Therefore what God has joined together, let man not separate.'

When they were in the house again, the disciples asked Jesus about this. He answered, 'Anyone who divorces his wife and marries another woman commits adultery against her. And if she divorces her husband and marries another man, she commits adultery.'

Jesus goes back to the origins of marriage in Genesis. The couple leave their families and become one unit. Jesus then says that there are no circumstances in which divorce is allowed.

This seems to contradict Matthew's and Luke's accounts of what was said. Some scholars suggest that Mark's version is the original teaching of Jesus, but that the early Christians found this too harsh. So when Matthew's and Luke's versions were written or edited they added the words 'except in adultery'.

John 2: 1–10

On the third day a wedding took place at Cana in Galilee. Jesus' mother was there, and Jesus and his disciples had also been invited to the wedding. When the wine was gone, Jesus' mother said to him. 'They have no more wine.'

'Dear woman, why do you involve me?' Jesus replied. 'My time has not yet come.'

His mother said to the servants, 'Do whatever he tells you.'

Nearby stood six stone water jars, the kind used by the Jews for ceremonial washing, each holding from twenty to thirty gallons.

Jesus said to the servants, 'Fill the jars with water'; so they filled them to the brim. Then he told them, 'Now draw some out and take it to the master of the banquet.'

They did so, and the master of the banquet tasted the water that had been turned into wine. He did not realize where it had come from, though the servants who had drawn the water knew. Then he called the bridegroom aside and said, 'Everyone brings out the choice wine first and then the cheaper wine after the guests have had too much to drink; but you have saved the best till now.'

A typical Jewish wedding is described here. It would have been a disaster to run out of wine. Mary seems to have rushed in offering help from Jesus, but he does not let her down. Usually, the cheap wine was used last – guests were drunk by then – but Jesus reversed the trend. He clearly approved of marriage and enjoyed a party or he would not have performed his first miracle there.

Activities

You have read the poem in Proverbs about a good wife.
a   Write a similar poem about a good husband in the twenty-first century.
b   If you have time, you could find out about a good husband 3000 years ago. **IT 1.1, C 1.2, 1.3, 2.3**

Exam questions to practise

Here are some sample exam questions from paper 2A. To help you score full marks, there are some tips from examiners for questions 1–3. Try to work out your own plan for answering questions 4 and 5.

1 Briefly outline one Bible passage that Christians might use to support their belief that divorce is wrong. (2)
   (NEAB 2000, B3a)

2 Explain one reason why some Christians may accept divorce. (2)
   (NEAB 2000, B3b)

3 What problems in their married lives might Christians face if they marry someone from another religion? (5)
   (AQA 2003)

Now try questions 4 and 5 on your own. Before you write your answers, spend some time thinking about your approach.

4 'It doesn't matter where you get married.' Do you agree? Give reasons showing you have considered more than one point of view. Refer to Christianity in your answer. (5)
   (NEAB 2000, based on B3d)

5 Explain how the Christian wedding vows help a couple to live their married life. Refer to the vows in your answer. (6)
   (NEAB 1999, C7a)

How to do well

1 Remember to state who said the words from the Bible. Also focus your answer on divorce. The commandment 'Do not commit adultery' will not gain marks if quoted on its own, because it does not say anything about divorce.

2 Use a Christian reason here, It is a short answer for only 2 marks, so you do not have time or space to go into detail. Give only one reason. Is there a Bible quote you could use?

3 This question is about marrying someone from another religion, not from a different branch of the Christian religion. Examples are Islam, Hinduism and Judaism. Think about family life and problems that might be more difficult if the couple are from different faiths.

Justice and reconciliation: love and forgiveness

Many people will say that you should forgive a person who has wronged you in some way. But that is easier said than done! The natural reaction is to take revenge or 'get even'. In this section we will look at what Jesus taught and what he actually did to live out his words. We will also consider what people aim to achieve by punishment.

This section includes:

- Crime and punishment
- Aims of punishment
- Capital punishment
- Fighting for human rights
- Bible passages 1
- Bible passages 2
- Exam questions to practise

Crime and punishment

It is not a **crime** to think wrong things.
It is a **sin** to think something wrong.
Bad thoughts can lead to crime.
It is also a sin to do a wrong action.

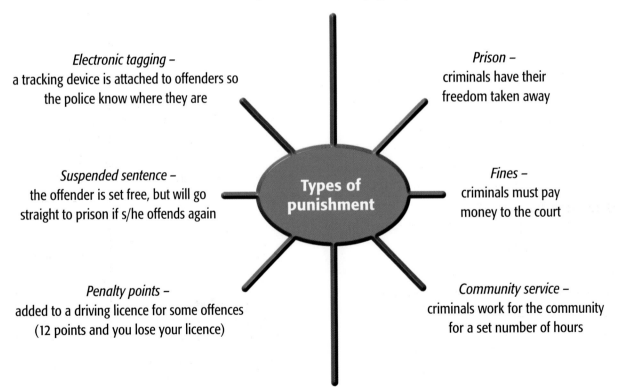

Capital punishment –
the killing of a criminal
(not used in UK; see page 58)

Electronic tagging –
a tracking device is attached to offenders so
the police know where they are

Prison –
criminals have their
freedom taken away

Suspended sentence –
the offender is set free, but will go
straight to prison if s/he offends again

Types of punishment

Fines –
criminals must pay
money to the court

Penalty points –
added to a driving licence for some offences
(12 points and you lose your licence)

Community service –
criminals work for the community
for a set number of hours

Loss of licence –
driving licence is taken away for an
offence like drink-driving

Why people turn to crime

There are lots of reasons why people might turn to crime, as the list below shows.

- The thrill of not getting caught.

- Poverty. (For some, crime is the only way to survive or have anything nice.)

- Some unemployed people say they get into trouble because they are bored.

- Drug addicts often commit crime to feed their habit.

- In some households crime is normal and the children do not regard it as wrong.

- People commit fraud because they want more money than they can legally earn or claim.

- Crimes of passion happen as a result of jealousy (for example, a husband may kill his wife's lover). These crimes are usually not planned in advance.

- Alcohol causes many crimes such as fights and drink-driving, because drunk people are unable to control themselves.

Youth Offending Teams

In 1998, there was a new act to change the way the courts treated young offenders (under eighteen). Every local authority had a **Youth Offending Team** (**YOT**). One aim was to identify the small number of young people who commit the largest number of crimes.

YOTs also aim to stop under-eighteens from offending. YOT members work closely with treatment centres for drug and alcohol action teams, and with local doctors, nurses, community police officers and local churches.

What crimes do under-eighteens commit?

- Violent assault on someone.

- Sexual offences.

- Reckless driving, often in stolen cars.

- Shoplifting.

- Burglary.

- Handling stolen goods.

- Drug-related crime.

- Race-related crimes.

- Fraud.

- Malicious damage to property.

Activities

1 Find out what the seven deadly sins are. Write down what you think each one means. Try looking on the Mission Research Corporation and the Deadly Sins websites for help by visiting www.heinemann.co.uk/hotlinks and clicking on this section. **IT 2.1, 2.2**

2 Divide a blank sheet of paper into three vertical columns.
   a In the first column, list all the different crimes you can think of.
   b In the second column, write down what you consider a suitable punishment for each crime.
   c In the third column, write down what the punishment would be in the UK today for each crime. **PS 2.1, 2.2**

Key points

- A sin breaks the law of God.

- A crime breaks the law of a country.

- A crime can be a sin – for example, murder. But a sin need not be a crime – for example, jealousy.

Aims of punishment

When a person is punished there is a reason behind it. There are five main **aims of punishment**, which means that there is an expected outcome after punishment such as reforming (changing) the person.

Five aims of punishment

- *Protection*. If the law puts offenders in prison, they cannot commit new crimes, like murder. This protects communities. It also means people cannot take the law into their own hands and attack criminals.

Prisons keep criminals away from the public.

Death Row: in the USA you can be put to death for killing someone else.

- *Retribution*. Taking revenge or 'getting even'. In the Old Testament there is the idea of 'an eye for an eye, a tooth for a tooth, a life for a life'. This means 'let the punishment fit the crime'. People who agree with capital punishment use this quotation to support their view.

- *Deterrence*. Here the idea is to punish criminals so that they decide not to commit the offence again. They do not want to return to prison. The other reason is to deter (put off) would-be criminals so that they decide not to offend because it is not worth the risk. An example is that drivers know they risk losing their licence if they drink and drive – so most do not do it.

- *Reform (rehabilitation)*. The hope is that criminals realize they have done wrong, are sorry and may try to put things right. They live as changed people. This is the Christian aim because Jesus taught his followers to forgive, not to seek revenge.

- *Vindication*. Communities expect offenders to be punished to show them they will not accept lawbreaking.

Reparation

Some people call this the sixth aim of punishment. The idea is to compensate the victim or the community for their loss or damage. This is the idea behind Community Service – working for others.

Some Christians make reparation. If they have done wrong they show they are sorry by giving money to charity or working in a charity shop.

Christian aim of punishment

One aim of punishment favoured by Christians is reform. This means that wrongdoers should understand what they have done wrong.

Jesus never said a person should not be punished, but he did forgive them their sins. He stressed that **repentance** means being sorry for what you have done wrong, putting things right and not making the same mistakes again.

The Sacrament of Penance

The Sacrament of Penance is one of the **sacraments** of the Roman Catholic Church.

The person who receives this sacrament is called the penitent. The penitent comes into the church and prays silently to God. The penitent then goes to the priest. The penitent tells the priest what he has done wrong. The priest may discuss the situation, then he gives a Penance. This usually fits the sin. For example, if the penitent has been greedy the priest may ask him to donate money to CAFOD.

The priest says the words of **absolution**: 'God give you pardon and peace and I absolve you from your sins.'

Results of Penance

- **Reconciliation** with God.
- Reconciliation with the church.
- A peaceful conscience.
- An increase of spiritual strength.

Act of Contrition (being sorry)

This is an example of a 'being sorry' prayer.

> Dear God,
>
> I am sorry for my sin; I admit what I have done. I will try to make up with those I have offended.
>
> Amen.

Activity

Which aim of punishment do you think is the most effective? List your reasons for thinking this. **C 2.1a**

Key points

- There are five main aims of punishment. It is difficult to select the most effective aim, as different things suit different people.
- There are ceremonies where you can openly show your repentance.
- Jesus never said you should not be punished.

Capital punishment

Most people have strong views on the death penalty, either for or against. Christians, too, have opinions. Both sides quote from the Bible to support their views.

Britain does not have a death penalty. Some states in the USA execute criminals, usually by lethal injection or the electric chair. Some countries kill people for political reasons without a trial. This is seen as the abuse of **capital punishment**.

The case for capital punishment

- Some Christians support capital punishment. They quote the Old Testament law of 'eye for eye', 'tooth for tooth'. Thus if you kill someone you should be killed.

- Some criminals are not sorry for their crimes (often murder). If they leave prison they will re-offend or might try to get revenge. Some rapists get a sexual thrill from stalking a victim. Some prisoners have to ask for protection from other prisoners.

- It is a deterrent. Others see the punishment and hopefully will not try to commit that offence.

- Some life prisoners ask to die rather than being kept in solitary confinement for their own safety. Many Christians say that being forced to be on your own is not **humane**.

- Some people say it is cheaper to kill a murderer and avoid using tax payers' money to pay for their upkeep.

- In countries like the UK 'life' rarely means life (dying in prison). So criminals get the chance to start again. But what about the relatives of victims?

The case against capital punishment

- Many Christians quote Jesus' teaching. He changed the old law of 'eye for eye' by saying, 'But I tell you: love your enemies.' Jesus then reversed the trend for revenge by saying, 'Turn the other cheek.'

- Other Christians argue that there would not be time for someone to repent.

- Once someone is executed you cannot bring that person back.

- Capital punishment is not a deterrent any more. In the USA there is no reduction in murders despite capital punishment.

- The executioner becomes a murderer.

- Some people become **martyrs** having died for their beliefs.

- Many Christians think that life is precious and God-given, so only God can end a life!

The Church of England's view

The Church of England last discussed the death penalty in 1983. It agreed that they would oppose the reintroduction of the death penalty in the UK.

ACLU death penalty campaign

Visit www.heinemann.co.uk/hotlinks and click on this section.

ACLU (American Civil Liberties Union) aims to end capital punishment in the USA. It says there are 3500 prisoners on **Death Row**. Many of these prisoners are black or **illiterate**. ACLU also says that many prisoners were homeless or very poor. They also had defence lawyers who were not very good. ACLU says that of every eight people sentenced to death, one was found 'not guilty'. Most of these were set free, but for some it was too late.

For the death penalty

Visit www.heinemann.co.uk/hotlinks and click on this section.

This pro-death penalty website was developed to give supporters of the death penalty information that is reliable.

The site proposes to list the murder victims in its database. It is estimated there will be about 6000 victims. The site will give their name, age and how they died, then the name of the murderer. It also gives up-to-date news items about murder and rape cases.

Activities

1   Which crimes do you think should be punished using capital punishment? Give reasons. **C 2.1a, 2.3, WO 2.3**

2   Relatives of murder victims can watch the killer die in the USA. Do you think this is right? What do you think Christians would say? Discuss in groups, then outline your reasons to the rest of the class. **C 2.1a, WO 2.2**

Key points

● Capital punishment (the death penalty) is an emotive (emotional) subject.

● There is teaching in the Bible used both for and against capital punishment.

● The USA still has the death penalty, but the police say there is no reduction in murders and that the death penalty is not a deterrent.

Here we look at the work of Amnesty International and Saint Maximilian Kolbe.

Amnesty International

Amnesty International campaigns for prisoners all over the world. Both Christians and non-Christians support its work.

Peter Benenson set up this group in 1961. He read about two students who were sent to prison for seven years for raising their beer glasses to support freedom for their country.

A Chinese proverb says: 'It is better to light a candle than to curse the darkness.' This inspired Benenson to make the picture of the candle wrapped in barbed wire, the symbol for Amnesty International.

Amnesty International's symbol

It is better to light a candle, than to curse the darkness.

Next, Benenson wrote a newspaper article called 'Forgotten prisoners: no charge, no trial'. He received 1000 letters of support in the first three days.

One year later ...

- Amnesty International had set up branches in seven countries.

- It was working on 210 genuine cases.

- It sent **delegations** to four countries to speak to their governments about individual cases.

And today ...

More than 40 years on, Amnesty International aims to be impartial and independent. Members do not get involved in cases in their own country. There are now over one million active members worldwide.

Examples of the work of Amnesty International

- Ending torture (working closely with Christians against torture).

- Trying to stop the illegal sale of British-made weapons to non-democratic countries, Eastern Europe and parts of Africa.

- A campaign to improve conditions in prisons.

- The campaign for all children to have basic human rights, including a ban on child soldiers. Some are only seven years old.

- Working in China to free students in prison. The Chinese government mowed down students who were lighting candles for peace and freedom in Tiananmen Square (China) and sent many others to prison (see page 77).

Saint Maximilian Kolbe

The story of Kolbe is an example of great sacrifice – giving your life to save others.

Kolbe was born in 1894 in Poland. He became a priest in 1918.

Kolbe soon came to realize that many people were against the Catholic Church.

In 1927, he set up a centre near Warsaw and sent leaflets to millions of people.

World War II began and the Germans attacked Catholics as well as Jews. In 1941, the Germans arrested Kolbe for being a Catholic and accused him of helping Jews. In May 1941, they sent Kolbe and 320 others to Auschwitz Concentration Camp.

There, Kolbe shared his rations with others, heard confessions and said **Mass**. He said, 'Hate is not creative. Our sorrow is necessary that those who live after us may be happy.' He always put others before himself to be treated by a doctor.

One day, a prisoner escaped. When he did not return by evening, the Commandant ordered ten men to die for the one who escaped. One man, Francis Gajowniczek, pleaded to be let off because he had a young family. Kolbe volunteered to take his place. 'I have no wife or children,' he said.

The ten men were sent to the starvation bunker. We know the details because the manager of the bunker wrote notes in his diary.

Not only was Kolbe wrongly imprisoned, he also gave his life to save another.

One by one the men died. But the soldiers noticed how calm the others were. Kolbe lead the remaining men in prayer.

Two weeks later there were only four men left and the Germans wanted the bunker for more men. They injected each man with carbolic acid and Kolbe had to watch. When it was his turn, he was calm. He raised his arm and after a second injection seemed to fall asleep. This was on 14 August 1941.

In 1982, Pope John Paul II made Maximilian Kolbe a Saint and Martyr of the Catholic Church. The family of the man whose life was spared attended the ceremony.

Activities

1 For many Christians, Kolbe is a martyr and a hero. But to some he is a fool. What do you think? List your reasons. **C 2.2**

2 Imagine you are Francis, the man who was spared. You have just been set free. You write a letter to your wife and children saying you are coming home. Give details in your letter about how your life was spared and what your feelings are. **C 2.2, 2.3**

Key points

- There are still many people throughout the world who are falsely imprisoned, without charge and without trial.

- Amnesty International and other groups campaign for the basic human rights of prisoners. They work in the spirit of reconciliation.

- Saint Kolbe was imprisoned and gave his life to save a fellow human being.

Here you will find the relevant Bible passages that you will need for the love and forgiveness section. The set passages are written out. Then there is an explanation of what they mean.

> **Jesus never said that you should not be punished. What he did say was we should forgive the sinner and give him a chance to reform.**

Set passages

Matthew 5: 38–48
(Teaching on forgiveness)

You have heard it said, 'Eye for eye, and tooth for tooth.' But I tell you, do not resist an evil person. If someone strikes you on the right cheek, turn to him the other also. And if someone wants to sue you and take your tunic, let him have your cloak as well. If someone forces you to go one mile, go with him two miles. Give to the one who asks you, and do not turn away from the one who wants to borrow from you.

You have heard that it was said, 'Love your neighbour and hate your enemy.' But I tell you: Love your enemies and pray for those who persecute you, that you may be sons of your Father in heaven. If you love those who love you, what reward will you get? Are not even the tax collectors doing that? And if you greet only brothers, what are you doing more than others? Do not even pagans do that? Be perfect, therefore, as your heavenly Father is perfect.

Jesus quotes the Old Testament principle of fair revenge but adds to it by saying, 'but I tell you do not take revenge'. Jesus turns the principle round. He goes on to talk about 'turning the other cheek'. This takes courage, as the natural human reaction is one of retaliation. Loving your enemies is difficult in practice, but Jesus makes clear he wants his followers to be different. They should 'stand out in the crowd'.

Luke 15: 11–32 (The forgiving father)

Jesus continued: 'There was a man who had two sons. The younger one said to his father, "Father, give me my share of the estate." So he divided his property between them.

'Not long after that, the younger son got together all he had, set off for a distant country and there squandered his wealth in wild living. He went and hired himself out to a citizen of that country, who sent him to his fields to feed pigs. He longed to fill his stomach with the pods that the pigs were eating, but no one gave him anything.

'When he came to his senses, he said, "How many of my father's hired men have food to spare, and here I am starving to death! I will set out and go back to my father and say to him: Father, I have sinned against heaven and against you. I am no longer worthy to be called your son; make me like one of your hired men." So he got up and went to his father.

'But while he was still a long way off, his father saw him and was filled with compassion for him; he ran to his son, threw his arms around him and kissed him. The son said to him, "Father, I have sinned against heaven and against you. I am no longer worthy to be called your son."

'But the father said to his servants, "Quick! Bring the best robe and put it on him. Put a ring on his finger and sandals on his feet. Bring the fattened calf and kill it. Let's have a feast and celebrate. For this son of mine was dead and is alive again; he was lost and is found." So they began to celebrate.

'Meanwhile, the older son was in the field. When he came near the house, he heard music and dancing. So he called one of the servants and asked him what was going on. "Your brother has come," he replied, "and your father has killed the fattened calf because he has him back safe and sound."

'The older brother became angry and refused to go in. So his father went out and pleaded with him. But he answered his father, "Look! All these years I've been slaving for you and never disobeyed your orders. Yet you never gave me even a young goat so I could celebrate with my friends. But when this son of yours who has squandered your property with prostitutes comes home, you kill the fattened calf for him!"

'"My son," the father said, "you are always with me, and everything I have is yours. But we had to celebrate and be glad, because this brother of yours was dead and is alive again; he was lost and is found."'

This parable is also called 'The prodigal son' or 'The lost son', but in this exam it is called 'The forgiving father'. It has several meanings:

- The father represents God and the story teaches us about how God loves to forgive. The father is waiting for his son, hoping that one day he will come home. God has given us free will. God waits for us, ready to forgive. When the son came home, the father celebrated. He didn't say, 'I told you so.'

- Christians learn about God who is the father. He is willing to forgive those who repent. Christians try to live like Jesus, so they too must forgive those who repent.

John 8: 1–11 (The woman in adultery)

Jesus went to the Mount of Olives. At dawn he appeared again in the temple courts, where all the people gathered round him, and he sat down to teach them. The teachers of the law and the Pharisees brought in a woman caught in adultery. They made her stand before the group and said to Jesus, 'Teacher, this woman was caught in the act of adultery. In the Law Moses commanded us to stone such women. Now, what do you say?' They were using this question as a trap, in order to have a basis for accusing him.

But Jesus bent down and started to write on the ground with his finger. When they kept on questioning him, he straightened up and said to them, 'If anyone of you is without sin, let him be the first to throw a stone at her.' Again he stooped down and wrote on the ground.

At this, those who heard began to go away one at a time, the older ones first, until only Jesus was left, with the woman still standing there. Jesus straightened up and asked her, 'Woman, where are they? Has no one condemned you?'

'No one, sir,' she said.

'Then neither do I condemn you,' Jesus declared. 'Go now and leave your life of sin.'

The key to the whole passage is, 'I do not condemn you either. Go but do not sin again.'

Bible passages 2

Set passages (cont.)

Jesus does not change the punishment for
adultery. But he says that nobody could throw
the first stone, because we have all sinned.
Jesus does not teach that one sin is bigger or
worse than another. He tells the woman not to
sin again, giving her a second chance.

Luke 23: 32–43 (The penitent thief)

Two other men, both criminals, were also
led out with him to be executed. When
they came to the place called the Skull,
there they crucified him, along with the
criminals – one on his right, the other on
his left. Jesus said, 'Father, forgive them,
for they do not know what they are doing.'

The people stood watching, and the rulers
even sneered at him. They said, 'He saved
others; let him save himself.'

The soldiers also came up and mocked
him. They offered him wine vinegar and
said, 'If you are the king of the Jews,
save yourself.'

There was a written notice above him,
which read: THIS IS THE KING OF THE JEWS.

One of the criminals who hung there
hurled insults at him: 'Aren't you the
Christ? Save yourself and us!'

The other criminal rebuked him. 'Don't you
fear God?' he said, 'since you are under the
same sentence? We are punished justly, for
we are getting what our deeds deserve. But
this man has done nothing wrong.'

Then he said, 'Jesus, remember me when
you come to your kingdom.'

Jesus answered him, 'I tell you the truth,
today you will be with me in paradise.'

The thief realized and accepted he was being
punished for his crime. He also knew that Jesus
was innocent. We are not told whether he
understood that Jesus was the Messiah or
God's son. But Jesus promised him that he
would remember him, and Jesus forgave him.

Matthew 18: 23–35 (The unmerciful servant)

The kingdom of heaven is like a king who
wants to settle accounts with his servants.
As he began the settlement, a man who
owed him ten thousand talents [special
coinage] was brought to him. Since he was
not able to pay, the master ordered that he
and his wife and children and all that he
had be sold to repay the **debt**.

The servant fell on his knees before him.
He begged, 'I will pay back everything.'
The servant's master took pity on him,
cancelled the debt and let him go.

But when that servant went out, he found
one of his fellow-servants who owed him a
hundred denarii. He grabbed him and
began to choke him. 'Pay back what you
owe me!' he demanded.

His fellow-servant fell to his knees and
begged him, 'Be patient with me, and I will
pay you back.'

But he refused. Instead, he went off and
had the man thrown in prison until he
could pay the debt. When the other
servants saw what had happened, they
were greatly distressed and went and told
their master everything that had happened.

Then the master called the servant in. 'You
wicked servant,' he said, 'I cancelled that
debt of yours because you begged me to.

Shouldn't you have had mercy on your fellow-servant just as I had on you?' In anger his master turned him over to the jailers to be tortured, until he should pay back all he owed.

This is how my heavenly Father will treat each of you unless you forgive your brother from your heart.

If we want to be forgiven by God and by others, then we must be prepared to forgive others, too, however small or big the sin.

The king represents God who forgives. The first servant is forgiven, but he is not prepared to do the same. God warns we will be punished for not forgiving.

Other relevant passages

Matthew 7: 1–5

'Do not judge, or you too will be judged …

Why do you look at the speck of sawdust in your brother's eye and pay no attention to the plank in your own eye? How can you say to your brother, "Let me take the speck out of your eye," when all the time there is a plank in your own eye? You hypocrite, first take the plank out of your own eye, and then you will see clearly to remove the speck from your brother's eye.'

Jesus tells us not to be too hasty to judge, criticize or condemn others. Sometimes it is called 'putting people down'. Jesus tells us to look at ourselves first and see what we have done wrong. We may well have done something more serious than those we are criticizing. This is what Jesus calls the 'plank'.

Matthew 6: 9–15

'This, then, is how you should pray:

"Our Father in heaven,
hallowed be your name,
your kingdom come,
your will be done
on earth as it is in heaven.
Give us today our daily bread.
Forgive us our debts,
as we also forgive our debtors.
And lead us not into temptation,
but deliver us from the evil one."

'For if you forgive men when they sin against you, your heavenly Father will also forgive you. But if you do not forgive men their sins, your Father will not forgive your sins.'

The prayer asks God to forgive us because we forgive others. Then Jesus explains we cannot expect to be forgiven if we will not do the same.

Activities

1 Do you agree that revenge is 'a natural human reaction'? Give reasons. **PS 2.1**

2 Imagine you are the penitent thief on the cross. Write down your conversation with Jesus, including your thoughts and feelings. End with Jesus forgiving you. How do you feel now? **C 2.3**

Exam questions to practise

Below are some sample exam questions for paper 2A. To help you score full marks, the first three questions are followed by some tips from examiners.

1 Explain why Christians disagree over the issue of capital punishment. You must use at least one Bible passage. (6) *(AQA 2003)*

2 Look at the picture below, then answer the questions that follow it.

 a What is the aim of punishment shown here? (1)

b What did Jesus teach to replace this attitude? (3)

c Explain one reason why it is hard to put Jesus' words into action? (2)

3 What can we learn about forgiveness from the parable of the forgiving father? (4) *(AQA 2002)*

Now try questions 4 and 5 on your own. Before you write your answers, spend some time thinking about your approach.

4 Think about the story in John 8: 1–11.
 a Why did the woman's accusers leave one by one? (2)
 b What did Jesus say to the woman that was important? (2)
 c What can Christians learn from this story? (2)
 (based on AQA 2002)

5 Explain why many Christians believe that reform is the most important aim of punishment. (5)

How to do well

1 Think about views for and against capital punishment. Then select one for and one against, which are Christian. You must include at least one Bible passage.

2 a Make sure it is an aim, not a type of punishment.
 b Think about what Jesus said, 'But I tell you …' There are three marks, so try to think of either three points or one statement well explained.

c You need to write down one reason, which will be worth one mark. Then you need to explain what it means, which is the second mark.

3 *Do not* rewrite the parable. You will gain few or no marks. Go through the main characters. How many are there? Try to write one thing about each person and maybe two about one of the characters. Make a list before you begin the essay.

Justice and reconciliation: war and peace

Every single day since World War II ended in 1945 there has been a war in some part of the world. In war there are at least two sides, usually each with a good reason for fighting. Countries – even poor countries – spend so much money on arms that often people starve for the sake of a war.

In this section we look at attitudes to war and ask questions such as 'Is war necessary?' We also look at alternatives to fighting. We ask 'What did Jesus say?'

This section includes:

- War: an introduction
- Just war
- Effects and cost of war
- Christians and war
- Pacifism and non-violent protests
- Peace and war crimes
- Aspects of war
- Nuclear warfare
- Bible passages 1
- Bible passages 2
- Exam questions to practise

War: an introduction

Key terms

War Armed conflict between two or more opposing groups.

Civil war People of the same country form opposing sides and fight each other. The reasons for this could be religious or related to different ethnic groups that make up the same country.

Holy War Fought with the belief that God is on their side and wants them to fight.

In **war** there are always at least two sides, both armed and with reasons why they are right to fight.

The nature of war has changed in the last 100 years. In World War I, there was trench warfare. Soldiers faced each other and charged at the opposite side. In World War II, aircraft dropped bombs on targets, and there were the first un-manned missiles. Now missiles can be launched from hundreds of miles away simply by pressing a button.

There are never any winners in war.

Until World War I, more than 90 per cent of casualties were men in the armed forces. Bombing in World War II by both Britain and Germany, however, killed millions of **civilians**. Some nations use civilians as human shields to protect their arms stores.

Sometimes the cause of a war may be something that happened hundreds of years ago.

Causes of war

- *Greed*. One country wants to gain land that has valuable resources, such as coal or oil.

- *Racial or ethnic problems*. Different racial or cultural groups find themselves living in the same country. They have serious differences that go back several generations. They may have religious differences. This can lead to **civil war**.

- *Religion*. Most religions teach about peace. Yet many wars are about religion – including civil wars. This happened in Ireland, India and Pakistan.

- *To stop a **tyrant/dictator***. A powerful country may support a weaker one to overthrow a dictator or to protect it against attack from another country.

Holy war

Holy wars are when people fight wars in the name of God. They believe God is on their side.

The Crusades of the Middle Ages were Holy wars. Christian Crusaders were fighting to make the Holy Land (Palestine) a Christian country. They fought against Muslims. Thousands of people from both sides died in the name of religion.

Peace-keeping: new role for troops

Towards the end of the twentieth century, troops had a new role. This was to act as peace-keepers on behalf of **NATO** (the North Atlantic Treaty Organization) or the **United Nations** (UN).

UN troops wear pale blue berets. The soldiers do not take sides. They try to keep the peace between two or more sides.

The UK sends troops to areas where there is unrest. Soldiers only fire their weapons in self-defence.

Some experts are concerned about the strain on UK resources. Thousands of troops went to Kosovo and Bosnia. They are likely to be involved for up to 20 years. A government advisor said: 'I have just come back from Bosnia and if the peace-keeping force left, the whole area would erupt.' (January 2001)

About 103,000 British troops are committed round the world. There are still 15,000 in Northern Ireland and 5000 in Bosnia. For the last year UK forces have been in Iraq. The UK had 7900 troops in southern Iraq in May 2004.

Many soldiers serving as peace-keepers suffer stress as a result of the horrible sights they have seen (committed by all sides).

The blue beret: a symbol of peace-keeping forces in troubled areas.

Activities

Using the Internet and reference books, make a list of the wars since 1945. (Archive newspapers are good to use. They can be found on newspaper websites.) For each war, list the following details.

a The names of the sides involved.

b What happened in the end **IT 2.3**

Key points

- War is complicated and caused by many factors.

- It is probably rare to find one side totally blameless.

- Historical factors often play a part in war.

Just war

'Just war' is a theory that attempts to justify wars and also tries to limit war. The first part of the theory was drawn up by St Thomas Aquinas, a Christian writer in the thirteenth-century Church. He was writing it with medieval wars in mind.

A thousand years ago

A thousand years ago the two armies camped either end of the chosen battlefield. On the battle day, the soldiers got into the formations following the orders of their commanders. A popular formation was:

- archers in front
- foot soldiers in the middle
- **cavalry** at the back.

When the trumpet sounded the archers began firing arrows. Then the rest charged. There was hand-to-hand fighting. The winning side was the one whose king survived or had the fewest casualties.

In medieval times, the side with the most troops still alive was the winner.

Modern warfare

From the earliest days, inventors were keen to make new weapons of war. In the twentieth century there were tanks, poisonous gas and fighting in the air. In World War II, both sides bombed civilian areas and submarines attacked merchant ships carrying supplies. Finally, the USA dropped the first **nuclear weapons** (bombs) on Japan.

Just war

St Augustine wrote two rules for a just war. Aquinas later added rule number three. From then on, Christians debated this topic and eventually there were five rules of war. (Some books say there are seven rules, as they divide them up differently.) It has been discussed whether all five conditions are required to make it a just war, or if only one is needed. No rule exists. Here are the five conditions of just war.

1 War must be started and controlled by a legitimate ruling authority (for example, a king who came to the throne as heir and not by murder or violence).

2 There must be a good (just) reason with a good chance of winning. An example could be sending troops to a small country that is being attacked by another big country.

3 War must be the last option after everything else such as talks, mediation and bargaining has been tried.

4 War must be to encourage good and overcome evil.

5 The country should use only the force necessary to bring about peace and achieve the aims of the war. Armies should not attack civilians.

War is only just if all other means of peaceful negotiation have failed.

From World War II onwards rule five has been ignored. Civilians have been the target of attacks to cause as much terror and misery as possible.

Laser-guided missiles: the weapons of modern warfare.

Saddam Hussein is facing trial for war crimes.

Effects and cost of war

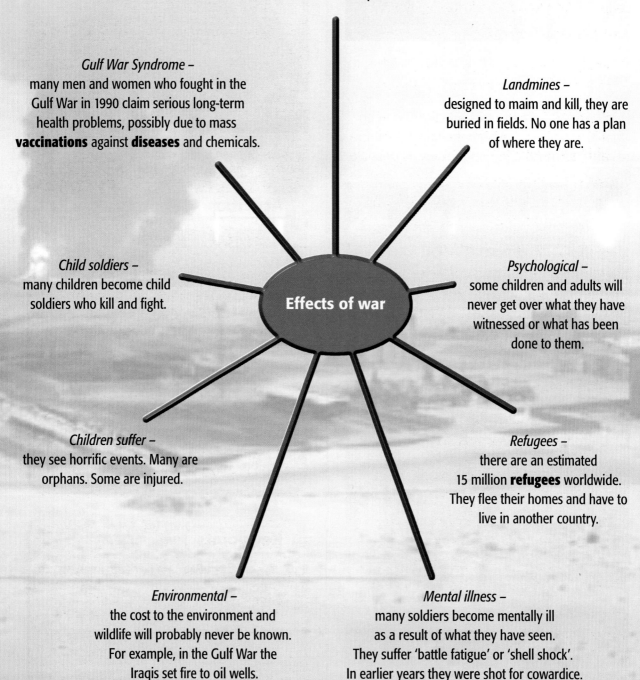

Ill health –
service personnel suffer from
long-term effects of gas, loss of
limbs, burns and depression.

Gulf War Syndrome –
many men and women who fought in the
Gulf War in 1990 claim serious long-term
health problems, possibly due to mass
vaccinations against **diseases** and chemicals.

Landmines –
designed to maim and kill, they are
buried in fields. No one has a plan
of where they are.

Child soldiers –
many children become child
soldiers who kill and fight.

Effects of war

Psychological –
some children and adults will
never get over what they have
witnessed or what has been
done to them.

Children suffer –
they see horrific events. Many are
orphans. Some are injured.

Refugees –
there are an estimated
15 million **refugees** worldwide.
They flee their homes and have to
live in another country.

Environmental –
the cost to the environment and
wildlife will probably never be known.
For example, in the Gulf War the
Iraqis set fire to oil wells.

Mental illness –
many soldiers become mentally ill
as a result of what they have seen.
They suffer 'battle fatigue' or 'shell shock'.
In earlier years they were shot for cowardice.

The arms race: right or wrong?

In the UK, keeping the armed forces equipped and up-to-date costs a lot of money. Millions of pounds are spent. In fact, in terms of expenditure, only the Health Service receives more. The British manufacture of weapons is a successful industry, employing more than one million people. Take a look at the following facts.

FACT £1.8 million is spent every minute all over the world on weapons.

FACT Europe and the USA spend more on weapons and armed forces than on **aid** to developing countries.

FACT For every fifteen years that a person pays tax in the UK, four of those years will have funded defence alone.

FACT War is the biggest cause of starvation, disability and poverty.

FACT A Tornado bomber costs £20 million minimum. Just think what that money could do for voluntary agencies in the UK and abroad.

FACT One guided missile costs almost £1 million. This money could send seeds, tools and experts to help 50 villages and solve their problems forever.

FACT Many smaller countries use banned chemicals instead of nuclear weapons.

FACT The cost of one jet fighter would vaccinate more than three million children against all major diseases.

Many Christians support the updating of weapons in the fear that if Britain is under-armed another country, perhaps seeking revenge, will attack. Others say that all events are controlled by God, so he will protect those doing his will.

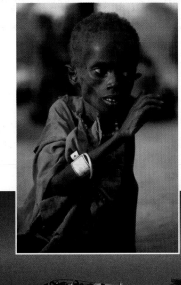

The real dilemma: is it better to fund war or a starving child?

Activities

1 Many civilian jobs depend on the armed forces. Make a list of some of these (for example, factories that make uniforms and boots). **PS 2.1**

2 The government has decided to spend less on defence. In groups of four or six imagine you are a committee asked to make a list of how you would spend the money saved. You could have up to ten schemes. Explain your choices. **C 2.1b, WO 2.1, 2.3**

Key points

- War is costly in many ways – in lost lives, in injuries, in psychological effects, in damage to the environment and in money.

- World poverty could probably be ended if armament spending was cut.

Christians and war

Some Christians believe there are good reasons for fighting a war. Others do not. Some say the teachings of Jesus do not really offer clear guidelines, because he never actually said that all wars are wrong.

Why Christians might fight

- They believe the reasons for war are right.

- St Paul says in Romans 13 that Christians must obey the government, who were put there by God. So if called up to fight then they must do so.

- They want to protect their families and relatives from being taken over by another country.

- Some people are **patriotic**. They are proud of their country and are willing to fight for their country.

- They might want to get rid of their government, which may be led by an unelected dictator/tyrant who took over by force.

Why Christians might not fight

- They might be **pacifists** who will not fight (see page 76).

- They might be **conscientious objectors** who will not fight in one particular war which they believe is wrong. They consider the arguments for and against the war.

- They do not want to die in battle. They do not want to kill, even in self-defence. They are afraid.

- It is a waste of resources and of people's lives.

- War causes suffering to families, and destroys valuable land and wildlife.

The cost of war is great on both sides.

Was Jesus a Pacifist?

There is no clear teaching in the New Testament to show whether Jesus was or was not a pacifist. He never actually said that war was wrong.

Jesus was not a pacifist

- Jesus drove out dishonest market traders from the temple (Mark 11: 15–18). He used a whip and is shown as very angry.

- Jesus never said war is wrong and that you should not fight.

- Jesus often quoted the Old Testament and then said 'but I tell you …' and proceeded to change it. He never changed anything about war, despite brutalities such as when armies entered a city and killed everyone, including the children.

- Simon the Zealot was one of the twelve disciples. The zealots wanted to fight against the Romans. They also ambushed small numbers of Roman soldiers and set their camps on fire.

- Jesus said the 'spirit of the Lord' was on him, and spoke about the need to release prisoners and set free those who are oppressed and persecuted (Luke 4: 16–21).

Jesus was a pacifist

- Jesus taught the idea of 'turning the other cheek', meaning no retaliation or 'getting even' (Matthew 5: 38–42).

- 'Blessed are the peacemakers' declares Jesus in Matthew 5: 9, adding 'they will be called sons of God' – in other words, they are very important people.

- When Jesus was arrested, questioned, beaten and sentenced to death, he put up no resistance (Matthew 26: 47–53). Peter got a sword to defend him, but Jesus said that violence breeds violence.

- When Jesus entered Jerusalem for the last time he rode in not on a horse as a warrior king but on a donkey, which is a symbol of peace.

- Jesus talked about how prisoners and enemies should be treated. He said they should be looked after properly. Then he added: 'Love your enemies.'

Activities

1 What would be your main reason for:
  a fighting in a war
  b not fighting in a war.

  Justify your responses. C 2.1a, PS 1.2

2 Note down why you think many teenagers want to join the armed forces. What is the appeal? You could find some recruitment posters and try to work out the facts behind the pictures and slogans. There are also several websites you could visit. C 2.3, IT 2.1

Key points

- Many Christians would have to think long and hard to decide if they would fight in war or not.

- Retaliation is a basic human reaction, so Jesus makes it clear what we should do.

- Christians who decide to fight might quote from Romans 13, which tells them to obey their government.

- Christians who decide not to fight might be pacifists or they might not think the cause is just.

- It remains undecided whether Jesus was a pacifist or not.

Pacifism and non-violent protests

Ideas about pacifism have developed over the centuries. Medieval Christian thinkers tried to square Jesus' and early Christian rejection of violence with the need to fight for political power.

Who are pacifists?

The Society of Friends (Quakers) are pacifists. They believe that there is something of God in all people, and that you must appeal to this inner ability to love and to do good. In 1661, their Peace Testimony was written. It said:

> The Spirit of Christ, which leads us into all truth, will never move us to fight war against any man with outward weapons.

In World War I, pacifists were treated as traitors. Officials sent those who refused to fight to the front line or had them shot. Others went to prison camps. Women sent white feathers (a symbol of cowardice) to known pacifists.

In fact, pacifists were not cowards. Many served in areas of great danger – for example, as stretcher bearers on the front line and as ambulance drivers.

White feathers are the symbol for cowardice. Yet pacifists were often brave for holding onto their beliefs.

Name:
Dietrich Bonhoeffer

Dates:
1906–1945

Country of birth:
Germany

Occupation:
Lutheran pastor

Life history

- Preached about pacifism in Nazi Germany up to 1939. Joined **non-violent protests** against Hitler.

- 1935–1940: helped Jews to escape to Switzerland. Travelled in the USA and Britain to spread information about **Resistance movement**.

- 1940–1944: involved with the Resistance. Realized Hitler would not respond to reason. Changed his beliefs about pacifism.

- 1944: took part in a plot to assassinate Hitler. Was arrested, beaten up and sent to prison in Berlin. Transferred to Flossenburg Concentration Camp.

- 9 April 1945: hanged as Allies approached.

Witness statement

'Bonhoeffer was brave, so composed, he died within seconds, obeying God's will.'

Last message

'This is the end for my body, but for me the beginning of life.'

Non-violent protest

This is an alternative to violent protest. Mahatma Gandhi used the idea to end British rule in India. Martin Luther King developed the idea to get civil rights for black people in the USA.

It is not true that no one ever gets hurt in non-violent protest. In China, tanks rolled over protesting students in Tiananmen Square. In South Africa, the army responded with water cannon, gas and bullets.

Examples of non-violent protest

- In Tiananmen Square in 1989, Chinese students held a candlelit vigil as part of a series of peaceful protests against lack of freedom in China, and to support democracy within China and other communist countries such as Russia. The Chinese leaders ordered army tanks to clear the Square. The protesters stood where they were. The tanks advanced. A young man refused to move, the tank moved on and rolled over the student.

- Many non-violent actions are dramatic – for example, people entering nuclear testing sites or entering air bases and sitting on the runway.

This brave civilian was mown down and killed by an army tank in Tiananmen Square.

- Shipbuilders in Nazi-occupied Denmark decided to 'misunderstand' orders (language problems!) and did their work so badly that the ships they were building were useless for war.

- Radio builders made mistakes, which meant the radios could only transmit or receive.

- Bomb factory workers built errors into the weapons, such as making them self-destruct.

What Christians believe

Christians accept that non-violent protest may achieve results slowly. Vaclav Havel was a Czech writer who was imprisoned for his political beliefs. However, due to popular non-violent action such as candlelit vigils, he was released, the government collapsed and he became the new president.

Activity

Act out the following role-play. You will need two people – a pacifist and his girlfriend.

The couple are discussing/arguing why the pacifist will not fight in World War II. The girlfriend is planning to send him a white feather with a picture of the two of them.

How do the conversations develop?

Practise the role-play, then act it out for the rest of the class. **WO 2.2, 2.3**

Key points

- Some non-violent protests make the headlines. Other tactics go on behind the scenes.

- It is not true that nobody gets hurt or killed. The protesters will aim for peace, but their opponents usually have the opposite attitude.

Peace and war crimes

Peaceful conflict resolution

Respect the right to disagree;
Express your real concerns;
Share common goals and interests;
Open yourself to different points
of view;
Listen carefully to all proposals;
Understand the major issues involved;
Think about probable consequences;
Imagine several possible alternative
solutions;
Offer some reasonable compromises;
Negotiate mutually fair cooperative
agreements.

The Festival Shop.

In the quiet of a Peace chapel, it is often easier to think about inner peace or say silent prayers.

Peace

Jesus taught his followers that peace is a sign of the **kingdom of God**. This is when there is no injustice, hunger or ill-treatment. It means everyone should learn to forgive, not to seek revenge. This is the key to peace.

Jesus said, 'Peace I leave with you' (John 14: 27). He also taught that no one should approach the altar to worship if they are angry with someone. They should make it up with that person first.

Inner peace and silent prayers

During **Holy Communion** Christians ask for inner peace when they pray for God's forgiveness of their **sins**.

They then continue: 'We meet in God's name: let us share his peace.' Then the congregation may 'share the peace' by shaking hands, or with a hug/kiss in some churches.

Many people visit city centre churches at lunch-time and go into a small chapel. Here they can feel calm, pray and find inner peace. They may also light a candle and pray for world peace.

War crimes

Some people say the only rule in war is to win. If there are no rules, there can be no crimes.

In 1945, the Nuremberg Trials started by writing down a list of war crimes. These included murder, deportation of civilians and killing hostages.

In 1949, the Geneva Convention wrote down rules about the treatment of enemy wounded and other prisoners. This included a list of war crimes, such as:

- killing, torture, doing experiments on prisoners

- deliberately causing suffering to the mind or body

- not giving prisoners of war a fair and public trial

- removal of civilians from their homes

- taking hostages.

In 1977 there were additions to this list, such as:

- using civilians as human shields (making civilians go to military targets and holding them in, for example, arms stores or weapons factories)

- delaying the release of prisoners of war

- not providing translators.

There were arguments about the meaning of words, but still, in the 1990s, further crimes were added to the list. These included rape, being forced to perform indecent or homosexual acts, beatings, mutilation and starvation.

Bosnia War Crimes Tribunal

This was the first such tribunal since the end of World War II. Bosnian Serb Dusko Tadic faced charges of the rape, torture and murder of prisoners in three prison camps in Northern Bosnia.

The trial took 78 days. It found Tadic guilty of eleven counts of beatings and persecutions. He was sentenced to twenty years in prison, with a minimum of ten years to be served.

Other Serbian war criminals

- Radovan Karadzic. Charged with putting thousands of non-Serbs into concentration camps and of **inhumane** treatment. He ordered snipers to fire on civilians. He captured 284 UN workers to use as human shields.

Dusko Tadic: a modern-day war criminal.

- Ratko Mladic. Charged as Karadic, but in addition he was charged with genocide. He ordered the massacre (killing) of over 6000 Muslim civilians.

- Slobodan Milosevic. President of Serbia. Charged with crimes against humanity and signing death warrants of thousands of people.

Activities

1 Do you think war criminals should receive the death penalty? Give reasons. **C 2.1a**

2 In your own words explain in detail the term 'war crime'. **PS 2.1, 2.2**

Key points

- Jesus taught about peace, including inner peace. He said that peace is a sign of the kingdom of God, and that the key to peace is forgiveness.

- Some people argue that there are no rules in war – you do what you can to win. Others argue that there are rules, and by breaking them you become a criminal.

Aspects of war

Key terms

Terrorism Use of violence or the threat of violence to create a climate of fear.

Terrorism

Terrorism is the use violence or threats to try to force political change. A number of terrorists in a group or 'cell' is usually small. They do not know the members of other cells.

Terrorists create fear by violence, which gains publicity. This raises their influence and power with the aim of change.

The last 50 years has seen a growth in terrorism – for example, the paramilitary groups in Northern Ireland, Arabs fighting Israel for land in Palestine and the events of September 11 2001.

Terrorists aim to kill people and destroy property. They may target civilians by bombing a bus or a pub, shooting at shoppers in a market or taking hostages. They cause fear and hope that the people will demand change. Sometimes the opposite happens and the people affected firmly resolve to defeat the terrorists. America made this resolve following September 11 and Britain chose to back them.

Freedom fighters and prisoners of conscience

Terrorists may call themselves **freedom fighters**. They may have a lot of popular support, because they believe their cause is right. For example, in South Africa the **ANC** (see pages 98–99) used terrorist acts to try to end **apartheid**.

Terrorist groups are bullies who try to frighten others into action on their behalf. This is Manchester, 1996.

Their leader was Nelson Mandela (see pages 98–99) who spent 25 years in prison. He said that:

- apartheid was evil

- the government was not democratically elected, as only the small white minority could vote

- all other options had been tried and failed.

Mandela felt his actions were right as, in the end, apartheid was ended. He became the first democratically elected president.

State terrorism happens in many South American and African countries. People who criticize or oppose the government are imprisoned without trial, tortured, beaten up, threatened, killed or simply disappear. They are sometimes called **prisoners of conscience**. Amnesty International campaigns on their behalf (see page 60).

Patriotism

Patriots are people who love their country and are proud of it (patriotic). They will often fly their national flag on special days. They sing their national anthem at public events, like football matches.

Nationalism

This is like **patriotism**, but **nationalists** go further. They may seek to separate from larger states, such as in the former states of the Soviet Union. They identify themselves as one particular kind of people and may hate 'foreigners' who live in their country (xenophobia).

They are prepared to attack or kill other groups. They have slogans such as 'Go home, foreigners. You don't belong here!' An extreme example is the ethnic cleansing by Serbs of whole populations because they were the 'wrong' race or religion.

Waving the flag, but is it harmless patriotism or the more sinister nationalism?

Activities

1 'Terrorism can never be right.' Discuss this statement in pairs, then write down your reasons for and against it.
   C 2.1a

2 Many people say they are patriotic. They might show this by supporting the national rugby or football team, by flag waving and attending. But football hooligans might also say they are patriotic. Is there a difference? Discuss in groups and list your reasons.
   C 2.1a, WO 2.2

Key points

- The use of terrorism is more widespread as groups try to force change.

- Nationalism can lead to a climate of fear and hatred of diversity.

Nuclear warfare

People are still suffering the effects today of a bomb dropped in 1945.

The atomic bomb

In August 1945, the USA dropped atomic bombs (**nuclear weapons**) on the cities of Hiroshima and Nagasaki in Japan. Half a million civilians died. Many more suffered the effect of radiation. Even today, women who were not even born in 1945, give birth to babies with defects.

Those who support the USA say the atomic bomb ended the war. It prevented further casualties and suffering.

Other nuclear weapons

Since the first atomic bombs, countries have made bigger, more deadly nuclear weapons. They also have missiles to deliver them.

In the 1980s, many countries signed a treaty banning the testing of nuclear weapons. In the 1990s, some Asian states and Pakistan tested weapons. This shows they now have the skills to make bombs.

Nuclear disarmament

- Nuclear **disarmament** means giving up nuclear weapons.

- Multilateral nuclear disarmament is when all countries get rid of their weapons at the same time.

- Unilateral nuclear disarmament is when one country gets rid of its weapons in the hope of encouraging other countries to do the same.

The Church and the bomb

The Church of England held a meeting in 1982, in which it said these things.

- It is the government's duty to keep enough armed forces to prevent 'nuclear blackmail'.

- Policy about war should only be for self-defence.

- It would never be morally right to use any kind of nuclear bomb.

- All countries should sign an agreement to say they would never be the first to use a nuclear bomb.

- Governments should destroy nuclear stockpiles.

Campaign for Nuclear Disarmament (CND)

Bruce Kent, a Roman Catholic priest and leader of CND.

CND began in 1958. Its logo, designed as an anti-nuclear symbol by Gerald Holton, is still used today and has become more commonly known throughout the world as the peace symbol. The aim of CND was to persuade the great powers, such as the UK, USA, Russia, France and China, to disarm. There was a great risk of accidents, with results that would be too awful to even think about.

In the 1980s, CND became popular again. Its leader was Monsignor Bruce Kent, a Roman Catholic priest. He gave up his ministry to work full-time for CND. He said that to use, or threaten to use, nuclear weapons was against Christian teaching about the **sanctity of life**. CND put forward its views about nuclear weapons, as follows.

- Countries like Japan have spent their money on industry rather than weapons, and have become very wealthy.

- The money spent on weapons could be spent on feeding starving people.

- The risk of nuclear accidents continues to rise. The consequences were seen at the Chernobyl nuclear power station accident in 1986 (see page 9).

New weapons of fear and death

In 2000, William Cohen, Defence Secretary of the USA, spoke about new fears. These were of attacks with chemical and biological weapons. Some countries were producing these in factories disguised as medicine factories.

These weapons are called **weapons of mass destruction** (WMD). They are quite cheap to produce, but are very destructive.

Saddam Hussein's troops gassed Kurdish villagers in Iraq using a nerve agent. The wind blew some of the gas into Iran, where other people died.

After the Gulf War of 1990, the UN ordered Saddam to destroy all his WMD. The suspicion that these weapons still existed in Iraq was one reason that led to the Gulf War in 2004.

Activity

Do you think it was right for Bruce Kent to give up the priesthood to lead a non-Christian organization? Give reasons.

C 2.1a

Key points

- The nuclear threat has lessened between the USA and Russia, but other countries might still use these weapons.

- The latest threat is weapons of mass destruction used by states who do not care that they are illegal.

Here you will find the relevant Bible passages that you will need for the war and peace section. The set passages are written out. Then there is an explanation of what they mean.

Set passages

Matthew 5: 38–48
(Teaching on forgiveness)

This passage is written out in full on page 62.

It is very easy to seek revenge when one person goes against another. It is just as much an issue when one country goes against another. Jesus is teaching Christians to be different and not do what everyone else does.

Jesus tells us to avoid situations that could lead to conflict. He sets us a difficult task. It is hard to walk away from violence and even more so to love your enemies.

Romans 13: 1–7
(The authority of the state)

Everyone must submit himself to the governing authorities, for there is no authority except that which God has established. The authorities that exist have been established by God. Consequently, he who rebels against the authority is rebelling against what God has instituted, and those who do so will bring judgement on themselves. For rulers hold no terror for those who do right, but for those who do wrong. Do you want to be free from fear of the one in authority? Then do what is right and he will commend you. For he is God's servant to do you good. But if you do wrong, be afraid, for he does not bear the sword for nothing. He is God's servant, an agent of wrath to bring punishment on the wrongdoer. Therefore, it is necessary to submit to the authorities, not only because of possible punishment but also because of conscience.

This is also why you pay taxes, for the authorities are God's servants, who give their full time to governing. Give everyone what you owe him: If you owe taxes, pay taxes; if revenue, then revenue; if respect, then respect; if honour, then honour.

Christians must be 'law abiding' citizens. God is in control and he put the ruler there.

Paul says if we disobey the ruler, we disobey God. If you break the law, then you deserve punishment. However, no ruler is entitled to make a person go against his or her conscience.

The problem with this passage is, what if the ruler goes against the Church? For example, in communist Russia, church services (except in some Orthodox churches) and using Bibles were banned. Many Christians broke the law of their land by just being Christian. They worshipped together in houses and some people smuggled in Bibles for them. The question was, should they break the law? And should they put others at risk by their actions?

Luke 4: 16–21

[Jesus] went to Nazareth, where he had been brought up, and on the Sabbath day he went into the synagogue, as was his custom. He stood up to read. The scroll of the prophet Isaiah was handed to him. Unrolling it, he found the place where it is written:

'The Spirit of the Lord is on me,
because he has anointed me
to preach good news to the poor.
He has sent me to proclaim freedom for
the prisoners and recovery of sight for
the blind,
to release the oppressed,
to proclaim the year of the Lord's favour.'

Then he rolled up the scroll, gave it back to
the attendant and sat down. The eyes of
everyone in the synagogue were fastened on
him, and he began by saying to them, 'Today,
this scripture is fulfilled in your hearing.'

Jesus is explaining a passage from the Hebrew
tenakh. Christians call it the Old Testament. It
was normal practice in a synagogue for a
passage to be read and a teacher (rabbi) to talk
about it.

Jesus is clear about his mission. He is there to
help the poor and the people that nobody
cares about. He will free prisoners and the
oppressed. Many Christians take this to mean
those who are wrongly imprisoned.

Matthew 26: 47–56
(The arrest of Jesus)

While [Jesus] was still speaking, Judas, one
of the Twelve, arrived. With him was a large
crowd armed with swords and clubs, sent
from the chief priests and the elders of the
people. Now the betrayer had arranged a
signal with them: 'The one I kiss is the man;
arrest him.' Going at once to Jesus, Judas
said, 'Greetings, Rabbi!' and kissed him.

Jesus replied, 'Friend, do what you
came for.'

Then the men stepped forward, seized
Jesus and arrested him. With that, one of
Jesus' companions reached for his sword,
drew it out and struck the servant of the
high priest, cutting off his ear.

'Put your sword back in its place,' Jesus
said to him, 'for all who draw the sword
will die by the sword. Do you think you I
cannot call on my Father, and he will at
once put at my disposal more than twelve
legions of angels? But how then would the
Scriptures be fulfilled that say it must
happen in this way?'

At that time Jesus said to the crowd, 'Am I
leading a rebellion, that you have to come
out with swords and clubs to capture me?
Every day I sat in the temple courts
teaching, and you did not arrest me. But
this has all taken place that the writing of
the prophets might be fulfilled.' Then all
the disciples deserted him and fled.

This passage can also be used in the section on
Love and Forgiveness. We are told by John that
it was Peter who wielded the sword. People
who support pacifism use this to show Jesus as
a man of peace, as he knew that violence
would lead to death.

The key point in this is 'All who take the sword
will die by the sword.' In today's language, this
could be interpreted as, 'Those who live by the
gun will die by the gun.' Summed up, it means
that violence causes more violence.

Activity

In groups, work out five examples of
occasions when Christians might decide it
is right to break the law of the land. One is
given in the explanation of Romans 13.
(Breaking the speed limit to get to hospital
isn't the sort of example needed here.)
WO 2.1, 2.3

Bible passages 2

Set passages (cont.)

Mark 11: 15–18
(The traders in the temple)

On reaching Jerusalem, Jesus entered the temple area and began driving out those who were buying and selling there. He overturned the tables of the money changers and the benches of those selling doves, and would not allow anyone to carry merchandise through the temple courts. As he taught them, he said, 'Is it not written:

"'My house will be called a house of prayer of all nations.'

But you have made it into 'a den of robbers'."

The chief priests and the teachers of the law heard this, and began to look for a way to kill him, for they feared him, because the whole crowd was amazed at his teaching.

Jesus was angry that traders and priests were cheating the poorest people who wanted to make sacrifices in the temple. Jesus took action and drove them out.

People who believe Jesus was a pacifist and those who think he was not both use this passage to support their ideas (see pages 74–75).

Those who think Jesus was a pacifist say that no one got hurt. He just overturned their tables and drove them out.

Those who think Jesus was not a pacifist say this is showing anger and the traders ran out before he hit them with a whip (another **gospel** says he picked up a whip). He showed 'justified anger'.

Other relevant passages

Micah 4: 1–3

In the last days
the mountain of the Lord's
temple will be established
as chief among the mountains;
it will be raised above the hills,
and the people will stream to it.

Many nations will come and say,
'Come, let us go up to the mountain of the Lord,
to the house of the God of Jacob.
He will teach us his ways,
so that we may walk in his paths.'
The law will go out from Zion,
the word of the Lord from Jerusalem.
He will judge between many peoples
and will settle disputes for strong nations far and wide.
They will beat their swords into ploughshares
and their spears into pruning hooks.
Nation will not take up sword against nation,
nor will they train for war any more.

Micah 5: 2–5

But you, Bethlehem Ephrathah,
though you are small among the clans of Judah,
out of you will come for me
one who will be ruler over Israel,
whose origins are from of old,
from ancient times.

Therefore Israel will be abandoned
until the time when she who is in labour gives birth
and the rest of his brothers return
to join the Israelites.

Micah looks into the future, to a time of peace when swords and weapons become farming tools. Disputes between nations will be resolved. Micah predicts the coming of the Messiah (the ruler over Israel) and describes him as a shepherd. Jesus often referred to himself as a shepherd, especially in John's gospel.

Isaiah 58: 6–10

Is not this the kind of fasting I have chosen:
to loose the chains of injustice
and untie the cords of the yoke,
to set the oppressed free
and break every yoke?
Is it not to share your food with the hungry
and to provide the poor wanderer with shelter –
when you see the naked, to clothe him,
and not to turn away from your own flesh and blood?
Then your light will break forth like the dawn,
and your healing will quickly appear;
then your righteousness will go before you,
and the glory of the Lord will be your rear guard.
Then you will call, and the Lord will answer;
you will cry for help, and he will say: Here am I.

If you do away with the yoke of oppression,
with the pointing finger and malicious talk,
and if you spend yourselves on behalf of the hungry
and satisfy the needs of the oppressed,
then your light will rise in the darkness,
and your night will become like the noonday.

God is concerned about the poor, the hungry and those who were treated unjustly. When peace comes the needs of everyone will be met. Isaiah talks about light in the darkness.

Romans 12: 9–21

Love must be sincere. Hate what is evil; cling to what is good. Be devoted to one another in brotherly love … Share with God's people who are in need. Practise hospitality.

Bless those who persecute you; bless and do not curse. Rejoice with those who rejoice; mourn with those who mourn. Live in harmony with one another. Do not be proud, but be willing to associate with people of low position. Do not be conceited.

Do not repay anyone evil for evil. Be careful to do what is right in the eyes of everybody. If it is possible, as far as it depends on you, live in peace with everyone. Do not take revenge, my friends, but leave room for God's wrath, for it is written: 'It is mine to avenge. I will repay,' says the Lord. On the contrary:

'If your enemy is hungry, feed him; if he is thirsty, give him something to drink. In doing this, you will heap burning coals on his head.'

Do not be overcome by evil, but overcome evil with good.

Paul repeats Jesus' teaching. He wants us to live in peace with everyone. He recommends we leave revenge to God, who judges. Instead we must look after our enemies – feed them, give them a drink, generally care for them. Paul says we must overcome evil with good.

Matthew 5: 9

Blessed are the peacemakers, for they will be called sons of God.

Jesus praises those who try to make peace. They are privileged and are called sons of God.

Activity

Reread the passages in this section. Then, in your own words, describe what world peace would be like. **C 2.1b**

Exam questions to practise

Below are some sample exam questions for paper 2A. To help you score full marks, the first four questions are followed by some tips from examiners. Before attempting the remaining two questions, try to work out your own plan. You will see that each of these is a high-scoring question. You will have to write longer answers.

1 Explain why some Christians believe that Jesus was a pacifist. (7)
(AQA 2003, C7a)

2 Explain the Bible teachings that might help a Christian decide whether to fight in a war or not. (6)
(based on AQA 2003)

3 In Romans 13, Paul tells Christians to obey their rulers and pay their taxes. What reasons does he give for doing this? (5)

4 Explain the conditions that need to be met for a Just war. You should include some examples. (8)

Now try questions 5 and 6 on your own. Before you write your answers, spend some time thinking about your approach.

5 'Terrorism is an example of Just war'. Do you agree? Give reasons for your answer showing you have thought about more than one point of view. (5) *(NEAB 2000, C7c)*

6 Look at the picture below.

a Explain how Christians could settle disputes between two countries without the use of violence. (6)

b Explain two drawbacks of non-violent protest. (4)

How to do well

1 Notice that this is worth seven marks. You must write enough to explain each point. A short answer will not gain many marks. You need to quote from the Bible in your answer.

2 This question is worth six marks. Explain in full each point you make. To gain high marks, you must use Bible passages.

3 Do not write out the passage word for word. Write in full sentences, not as a numbered list or in bullet points.

4 This will be quite a long answer. Again, write in full sentences, not in a numbered list or bullet points. To gain high marks you must give examples.

Christian responsibility: prejudice and discrimination

Prejudice is a biased way of thinking. Discrimination is putting these thoughts into action. People commit terrible crimes because of prejudice. People suffer not just because of their race or colour. They may suffer because of attitudes to gender, disability, religion and social class.

This section looks at a number of issues involving prejudice and discrimination, and the way Christians respond. It also looks at what the Bible says, and the lives of famous Christians who fought against discrimination.

This section includes:

- Prejudice and discrimination: an introduction
- Types of prejudice and discrimination
- Jesus and discrimination
- Christian attitudes to women in Britain
- Nelson Mandela
- Archbishop Desmond Tutu
- Martin Luther King
- Bible passages 1
- Bible passages 2
- Exam questions to practise

Prejudice and discrimination: an introduction

Key terms

Prejudice Pre-judging – that is, having a biased feeling or attitude about a person or a group of people before you know the facts.

Discrimination Prejudice in action. It is acting differently towards someone because of, for example, his or her colour, race, gender or disability.

The law

In the UK, **discrimination** is now against the law. However, it is one thing to change the law, and another to change attitudes.

The Race Relations Act 1976 made it illegal to discriminate on the grounds of colour, race or nationality in the areas of employment, housing and education. The aim was to enable people of different races to live side by side. The Commission for Racial Equality (CRE) was set up to deal with cases of discrimination.

The Amendment Act of 2000 aimed to strengthen the 1976 Act. It introduced new areas where discrimination was illegal. These were hospitals, schools, local councils and government departments.

- Local authorities could be prosecuted if they discriminated against anyone.

- Chief Officers of the police were responsible for their officers.

- The government was not to discriminate when making public appointments or awarding honours.

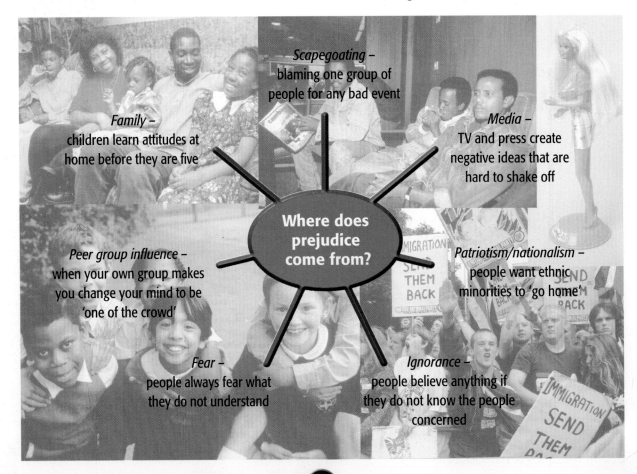

Where does prejudice come from?

Scapegoating – blaming one group of people for any bad event

Family – children learn attitudes at home before they are five

Media – TV and press create negative ideas that are hard to shake off

Peer group influence – when your own group makes you change your mind to be 'one of the crowd'

Patriotism/nationalism – people want ethnic minorities to 'go home'

Fear – people always fear what they do not understand

Ignorance – people believe anything if they do not know the people concerned

Even guide dogs for the blind sometimes suffer discrimination.

- *The Equal Pay Act 1975* stated that women were to be paid the same as men if doing the same (or a broadly similar) job.

- *The Sex Discrimination Act 1975* meant that it became illegal for an employer to specifically advertise that men or women were required for a job. There are exceptions; a carer of a disabled or elderly person may advertise for a female, for a female patient or male, for a male patient. Women had to have the same opportunities as men for promotion.

- *The Disability Discrimination Act 1995* aimed to help those with disabilities. Disability is defined in this act as anyone who has a physical or mental impairment which has a substantial and long-term effect on his or her ability to carry out normal day-to-day activities. You do not have to be registered disabled to qualify.

The Act gave disabled people new rights in employment, housing, transport and education. Public buildings had to ensure disabled people had suitable access. Churches and church halls also had to make alterations to include ramps, new toilets and suitable seating.

In 1999 'Information provision' became law. This meant that information from agencies providing any kind of service should have it available in Braille or on audiotape. (An example is a bus timetable.)

Blind people hope that discrimination against guide dogs will also be covered – for example, taxis must now carry guide dogs free of charge.

Activities

Using the Internet, look up one of the acts on pages 90–91. Then answer the following questions.

a Why was it necessary to have such an act?
b What did it set out to do?
c Has it been successful in its aims?
IT 1.1, 2.2

Key points

- Children are influenced from birth and learn **prejudices** before they even reach school.

- Two of the biggest causes or prejudice are fear and ignorance of someone you have never met.

- There have been several Acts of Parliament about discrimination.

There are many different types of prejudice and discrimination.

- *Racism* is discrimination against someone because of his or her race. Below is a list of race categories found on many forms.

White	British
	Irish
	any other white
Mixed	white and black Caribbean
	white and black African
	white and black Asian
	any other mix
Asian/Asian British	Indian
	Pakistani
	Bangladeshi
	any others
Black/Black British	Caribbean
	African
	any others
Chinese	
Other ethnic group	

- *Colour discrimination* is treating people differently because of the colour of their skin.

- *Religious discrimination* is treating people differently because of their religion. Some times it depends on which **denomination** these people belong to.

- *Disability discrimination* is treating people differently because they are disabled.

- *Gender discrimination* is treating someone differently because of their sex (gender) – that is, whether they are male or female. It is also called **sexism**.

Examples of discrimination

- *Racism*. A landlord tells a man who is Asian British that the room he would like to rent is taken – even though it is not.

Is it fair that you should be discriminated against simply because of your race?

- *Colour discrimination*. A PE teacher and two boys tell a black British boy he should be able to run quicker. They said black people can run fast.

- *Disability discrimination*. An adult in a wheelchair who works full-time and lives with his wife and children finds he cannot get into buildings and kerbs are too high. Someone else has to go with him. At the cinema they limit the number of disabled people who can go in – he is a 'fire hazard'!

How would you feel if you were considered a fire hazard?

- *Gender (sex) discrimination.* A well-qualified woman applies for a job at an insurance company. Although she is the best person for the job, she is not offered it. The owner is male and he believes that working women are not reliable because they might need extra time off work to care for their children when they are ill.

  In 2003 women were still earning, on average, 17 per cent less than their males colleagues.

Results of prejudice and discrimination

Prejudice leads to discrimination, because most people act on their thoughts. People are attacked and sometimes the attack ends in murder. There were 48,000 race crimes in England and Wales in 2000. Some people, including children, are driven to **suicide**. Rumours become fact. One tragic result is genocide, when someone decides to murder a whole race (for example Hitler had six million Jews killed).

Church of England policy

In 1985, an important report by the **General Synod** called 'Faith in the City' was published. The report made it quite clear that racism was still present in society. In 1989, a further report was published. It concluded that children should be taught positive race ideas while still at playgroups.

The Synod published two books on racism: *Seeds of Hope* and *Passing Winter*.

Activities

1   Which kind of discrimination do you think is the worst? List your reasons. **PS 2.1**

2   Try to explain what is meant by the term 'positive discrimination'. **PS 2.1, 2.2**

Key points

- Prejudice is the thought; discrimination is the action.

- There are many types of discrimination, not just racism.

- The result of prejudice and discrimination is always going to hurt someone and, at its worst, can cause **war** or death.

Jesus and discrimination

Key terms

Leper A person suffering from leprosy, a disfiguring skin disease. Lepers were treated as outcasts.

Jesus chose a Samaritan as the hero of his parable of the good Samaritan (Luke 10: 25–37) to show who our neighbours are. The listeners would have expected the Samaritan to kill the wounded man. You can almost imagine the gasps of horror when Jesus finished the story!

Sometimes it can be very hard to overcome prejudice and deal with real people in real situations. Here are some examples.

- You get a good job, good pay and conditions, and good chances of promotion. Then you find out the owner of the company is homosexual and lives with his partner. What would you do?

- You get very friendly with a boy or girl by chatting on the Internet. You know you live quite close by. You share a joke, a laugh, and then agree to meet up. At that meeting, it turns out the person is a different colour to you. What do you do?

Jesus and race

In Luke 7: 1–10 (the Centurion's servant) the centurion, a Roman, recognized the greatness of Jesus as he walked towards his house. He believed Jesus could heal the servant from where he was. Jesus did heal the servant from a distance. Jesus said: 'I have not found such great faith even in Israel.' He praised the faith of a foreigner, a **gentile**.

Jesus and religion

Jews hated the Samaritans. And Samaritans hated the Jews. Jews regarded Samaritans as having **corrupted** the Jewish religion by marrying local people.

Jesus and women

In the time of Jesus, it was not considered right for men to speak to women unless they were related – and even then, it was in the privacy of the home.

Women were expected to care for children. Unmarried women, or wives who could not have children, were pitied. This did not bother Jesus. He spoke to a Samaritan woman and ended up changing her life (John 4: 5–10, 27–30).

Two of his best friends were Martha and Mary, sisters of Lazarus. Jesus often went to their home it seems to find peace and quiet. He let the sisters listen to him, rather than just allowing them to serve him.

When Jesus was crucified, the women followers gathered round. And when he rose on Easter Day it was to women that Jesus first appeared.

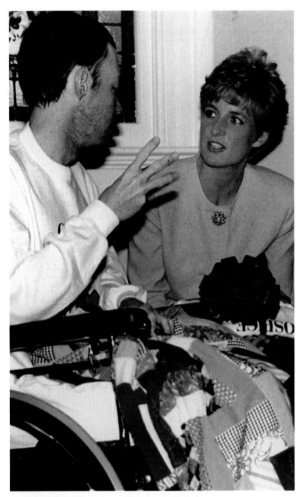

AIDS cannot be caught by shaking hands.

Jesus and disability

At the time of Jesus, most people believed that if you became ill God was punishing you for sin. If you were born disabled, then God was punishing your parents for some great sin. That was why Jesus forgave sins when he healed people.

Jesus felt sorry for people who suffered disability or illness. He healed them. When he healed **lepers**, he spoke to them and touched them. This was unheard of in his day. This is like when Princess Diana held hands and hugged **AIDS** patients.

When Jesus healed blind people, he let them feel his hands and face first and he told them what he was doing. With deaf people he often wrote for them using a stick in the sand.

Activity

Imagine you are a leper. Write a letter to a friend explaining how Jesus treated you. Include your feelings and what you think about Jesus. **C 2.2, 2.3**

Key points

- Jesus dealt with all types of people, from high ranking to the lowest.
- Jesus disregarded tradition or etiquette if it interfered with his ministry.
- Jesus understood the needs of may different groups of people.

Christian attitudes to women in Britain

The debate about women priests is almost as heated as that surrounding **abortion**. Some denominations accept women fully, some accept them partially and some do not accept them at all. The United Reform Church accepts women ministers. The Anglican Church differs from area to area. The Roman Catholic Church does not accept women priests at all.

The Anglican Church

By 1998, the Anglican Church ordained women priests except in some male-only areas in parts of Asia and Africa. In some parishes in England,

the church council decided that it would not accept a female priest.

Some male priests threatened to leave the Anglican Church in response and become Roman Catholic. Some male priests did leave, but if they were married they could not become Roman Catholic priests.

The Roman Catholic Church

The Roman Catholic Church still does not ordain women to be priests. It gives many reasons for this.

Arguments for and against women priests

Against

- Jesus chose twelve special male disciples and commissioned them to go out into the world, but no female ones.
- Paul taught that women should be silent in church (1 Corinthians 14: 34–35) and should not teach men (1 Timothy 2: 12).
- The ministries of women mentioned in the New Testament had nothing to do with the **sacraments** (consecrating Holy Communion).
- The church fathers rejected women priests in every debate.
- Medieval church law again excluded women priests.
- From the earliest times it has been practice not to ordain women to the priesthood, thus it is tradition.
- In the **Mass**, the priest takes on the role of Christ, which a woman cannot.

Counter arguments

- Priscilla (Acts 18: 26) and Phoebe (Romans 16: 1) are mentioned in terms of a teaching ministry and leadership.
- Paul is known for his dislike of women, and his ideas applied to how women were regarded in his society.
- The church fathers were prejudiced before the debate began.
- Medieval church law was based on the law of the founders.
- Tradition was based on prejudice against women.
- The priest is re-enacting the Last Supper. When Jesus said, 'Do this to remember me' he did not say 'only men must do this because I only had twelve male disciples with me'.

Women priests: the right or wrong thing to do?

Other reasons why women may become priests

- In **baptism**, women and men share equally in the death and resurrection of Jesus. The Holy Spirit descends on men *and* women.

- The male-only attitude is sexist.

- It is known that until the ninth century AD the Church ordained women to become deacons.

- Other denominations have studied and prayed, and they now ordain women as priests. This must be the mind of Christ.

Comments from men about women priests

'Women are suited to the ministry just as men are. You get good and bad vicars whether male or female.'

'I will not receive **Holy Communion** from a woman.'

'I thought at first I would hate a woman vicar, but in my last church there was one and she was the best thing that ever happened to that church.'

Comments from women about women priests

'Women vicars would be better with young children.'

'I prefer a male vicar. But if a woman was all that was available I would be OK about it.'

'I think they'd be sympathetic to people with problems, or who are sick or bereaved.'

'I hate women priests wearing a shirt and clerical collar, imitating men. They should design their own.'

Activities

1 Find out which denominations allow women priests and which do not. **PS 1.1**

2 What are your opinions about women priests? **PS 1.1**

3 If a church does not allow women priests, does this mean its members are prejudiced? **PS 2.1, 2.2**

Key points

- The issue of women priests has been hotly debated.

- Women can become priests or ministers in most denominations.

- Women cannot become priests in the Roman Catholic Church.

Nelson Mandela

Three Christians who have worked against racism are Nelson Mandela, Archbishop Desmond Tutu and Martin Luther King. In the next few pages, we will look at each of these people.

Influences on Mandela

In South Africa there was a system in place called **apartheid**. This meant that people were separated according to their colour. Black people had no rights, no vote, no proper jobs, bad housing on the worst land and no running water.

They had to carry passes, were often imprisoned and were kept separate from whites in everything. Even park benches were labelled for white or black use.

The ANC

The **ANC** (African National Congress) was founded to fight for black rights. The proportions of people living in South Africa were as shown in the pie chart opposite.

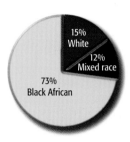

15% White

12% Mixed race

73% Black African

Mandela joined the ANC in 1944 and tried to set up talks with the government. He was convinced that apartheid was wrong and that the Bible supported his view. Mandela decided there was no option but to use violence. This was a necessary evil to defeat a greater evil. In 1963, Mandela and several of his friends were arrested, charged with trying to overthrow the government and sentenced to life imprisonment.

Nelson Mandela

'I have cherished the ideal of a free society in which all persons live together in harmony and equal opportunities. It is an ideal which I hope to live for, but if need be, it is an ideal for which I am prepared to die.'

1918	Born in South Africa.
	Grew up as a **devout** Methodist.
	Trained as a black lawyer in Johannesburg.
1944	Joined the ANC and tried to negotiate in the name of Christ's peace.
1963	Was sentenced to life in prison on Robben Island.
	Continued his campaign in prison and worked to help his fellow prisoners.
1980s	Worldwide campaign to end apartheid and free Mandela.
February 1990	Mandela was freed.
1994	Became the first democratically elected president of South Africa.
June 1999	Retired.

Freedom

Few countries would trade with South Africa. Also, their sporting teams and athletes were banned from international events.

In 1989, President Frederick Willem de Klerk came to power. He called for talks to work out a new constitution. On 11 February 1990, Mandela was set free after 27 years in prison. In 1994, there were free elections and Mandela became the first democratically elected president of South Africa.

Problems

Mandela began the slow process of healing wounds, teaching people to forgive and to work together. His aim was to redistribute wealth. He had to start from scratch, building multi-racial schools and beginning to reclaim areas from white people. He nationalized services such as the electricity supply.

Mandela did a tremendous public relations job. He visited **boycotting** countries and persuaded them to trade, invest or work in South Africa.

Many books have been written about Mandela. He wrote his autobiography called *Long Walk to Freedom*.

Extracts from Mandela's autobiography

The dark years

Time may stand still for those of us in prison but it did not halt for those outside. I was reminded of this when I was visited by my mother in the spring of 1968 … my mother suddenly seemed very old … My mother had lost a great deal of weight, her face appeared haggard.

I looked back and evaluated my own life. Her difficulties, her poverty made me question whether I had taken the right path – had I put the people's welfare before that of my own family?

Freedom

I went on stage about nine o'clock. Mrs King, wife of Martin Luther King, was on the podium that night as I said: 'This is one of the most important moments in the life of our country. Now with joy we can loudly proclaim "Free at last!" I stand before you humbled by your courage … I am your servant … This is a time to heal the old wounds and build a new South Africa.'

Activities

1 List the reasons that made Nelson Mandela work against apartheid. **C 1.2**

2 What has Mandela achieved? **PS 2.1**

Key points

- Mandela's dilemma was whether he should use violence or not.

- He and his supporters say his choice of violence was the right one.

- Problems still remain in South Africa. There are still huge inequalities.

Archbishop Desmond Tutu

Archbishop Desmond Tutu

'My vision is of a South Africa that is totally non-racial. A new South Africa, a free South Africa, where all of us, black and white together, will walk tall, will hold hands as we stride forth ... human beings made in the image of God.'

1931	Born in South Africa. Educated in the school for black children. Trained as a vicar after gaining his teaching diploma.
1961	Ordained as priest.
1962–1965	Studied in the UK. Lectured in South African universities.
1976	Became Bishop of Lesotho. Worked for peace.
1984	Won Nobel Peace Prize.
1985	Became Bishop of Johannesburg.
1986	Became Archbishop of Cape Town. Used his position to campaign against apartheid.
Other details	Always advocated non-violence.

Influences on Tutu

As a black child Tutu struggled to gain an adequate education. After studying he became a priest in 1961 – first working in London, then lecturing throughout South Africa.

Tutu preached against apartheid. The police and some fellow priests told him he should keep out of politics. He replied: 'I am puzzled as to which Bible people are using when they suggest that religion and politics do not mix.'

Dilemma

Tutu faced a dilemma: he opposed apartheid, but the Army and the police supported it. If you opposed them, they would charge you as a terrorist or communist. They might torture you, imprison you or execute you. He questioned whether violent or **non-violent protest** was right.

In 1976, he became bishop of Lesotho, gaining some authority. By then he had chosen to lead the non-violent struggle using marches, boycotts and petitions. He drew attention to his actions by inviting the world's **media** to events. For example, the BBC filmed state police attacking unarmed children.

Nobel Peace Prize

In 1984, Archbishop Tutu gained the Nobel Peace Prize. In his speech he said: 'I will not be told by secular authorities what **gospel** I must preach!'

In 1985, he was Bishop of Johannesburg. He again denounced apartheid as one of the 'most vicious systems since Nazism; the day I am proved wrong I will burn my Bible, the source of all teaching'.

Desmond Tutu receiving the Nobel Peace Prize.

Mandela chose Tutu to lead South Africa's Truth and Reconciliation Commission. This was a group of men and women chosen to investigate crimes committed by all sides during apartheid. Tutu was appalled at the evil uncovered on all sides, but believed it was necessary to try to heal damaged, wounded people.

Desmond Tutu is extremely ill at the moment. He is dying of cancer, but nurses say he never complains.

LEARN from the PAST; LIVE in the PRESENT; PLAN for the FUTURE!!!

Archbishop

Desmond Tutu became the first black Anglican Archbishop of Cape Town in 1986. He remained humble. His personality radiates God's love and even the most hardened soldier finds it hard to remain unmoved. His opposition to apartheid comes from his simple faith. He is a man who studies his Bible daily, prays and worships God.

Archbishop Tutu always opposed violence. He said: 'If you use violence I will find it difficult to speak for the cause of liberation. You cannot use methods that our enemy will use against us.'

End of apartheid

Archbishop Tutu's work did not stop with the end of apartheid. He continues to speak out against injustice. He is called 'the voice of the forgotten' – that is, the poorest people, children and other minorities.

Activity

List the reasons why you think it took so long to end apartheid, despite the use of violence and non-violence. **C 1.2**

Key points

- Archbishop Desmond Tutu is seen as the opposite of Mandela, although they are both Christians.

- Mandela decided that violence was needed. Tutu chose non-violence, preaching a gospel of **reconciliation**.

- Tutu's belief in God kept him going. He believed the Bible taught him all he needed to know.

Martin Luther King

Martin Luther King

'I have a dream that one day this nation will rise up and live out the true meaning of its creed. We hold these truths to be self-evident that all men are created equal. I have a dream that my four little children will one day live in a nation where they will not be judged by the colour of their skin but by the content of their character.'

1929	Born in Georgia, USA.
1948	Ordained a pastor of Baptist church.
1955	Bus Boycott began his active campaign against racism.
1961	Led series of sit-ins and rallies, which gained coverage throughout the USA.
1964	Achieved Civil Rights Act, some segregation ended.
1965	Voting Rights Act, black people had same voting rights as white.
4 April 1968	Murdered by James Earl Ray, who claimed he had been set up.
Other details	King always advocated non-violent protest – 'meet hate with love'.

Influences on King

When Martin Luther King was born in 1929, the USA, especially in the South, operated **segregation** against black people with separate schools, transport systems and churches.

The 1950s

Martin Luther King learned about Mahatma Gandhi and his writings on non-violence. King started to speak out against segregation and the oppression of black people. He became involved with the Bus Boycott in Montgomery in 1955, when black people stopped using buses until they were treated equally.

In 1957 King continued to preach non-violent direct action including marches, boycotts and sit-ins. More white people joined his campaign.

The 1960s

In the early 1960s King led demonstrations against segregated housing, hotels, restaurants and transport. Many white businesses never recovered from the loss of trade.

In 1963, King organized a march of hundreds of school children aged up to sixteen years in downtown Birmingham (USA), to protest against inferior schooling for black children. They were singing, chanting and waving home-made banners. King invited the world's press. The police commissioner sent police with attack dogs and water hoses to end the march. Scenes of children being attacked by dogs and being knocked down by pressure hoses were shown on TV and in newspapers worldwide.

In 1965, King campaigned for equal voting rights. The police broke up a peaceful march using tear gas and beatings. King made sure the event was televized. That year, the Voting Rights Act enabled black people to vote.

Violence erupts

By the mid-1960s young black people began to question King's objection to violence. The Black Power group formed and looked to Malcolm X, a black Muslim leader who argued for the rights of black people to use violence against attack. The Ku Klux Klan, a secret terrorist group who hated black people and often burned them alive, counter-attacked.

The Ku Klux Klan hated black people.

Assassination

Martin Luther King was murdered by James Earl Ray on 4 April 1968. King once said: 'When I die my work will only just be beginning.'

The third Monday in January is now a national holiday in the USA in honour and memory of King. More and more black people campaigned for rights and won them. Black people now have important jobs, such as the black former Mayor of New York, and Jesse Jackson, who stood for president.

Jesse Jackson: he might not be in a position of power had it not been for the work of Martin Luther King.

Activities

1 Do you think it was right of King to continue his campaign despite the danger to his wife and family? Give reasons for your answer. **C 2.1a**

2 Read the quote below.

> We can only see with open eyes,
> We can only listen with open ears;
> We can only think with open minds.

a Explain what you think is meant by 'open eyes', 'open ears' and 'open minds'.

b List how you feel this fits with King's character. **C 1.1, 2.1a**

Key points

- King felt led by God to use his public speaking skills and charismatic personality to lead campaigns against racism.

- In all areas King chose non-violent action. His motto was, 'Meet hate with love'.

- Most of his achievements probably happened after his death, when it became more acceptable for black people to take office.

Here you will find the relevant Bible passages that you will need for the prejudice and discrimination section. The set passages are written out. Then there is an explanation of what they mean.

Set passages

Luke 10: 25–37 (The Good Samaritan)

On one occasion an expert in the law stood up to test Jesus. 'Teacher,' he asked, 'what must I do to inherit eternal life?'

'What is written in the Law?' [Jesus] replied. 'How do you read it?'

He answered: '"Love the Lord your God with all your heart and with all your soul and with all your strength and with all your mind"; and, "Love your neighbour as yourself."'

'You have answered correctly,' Jesus replied. 'Do this and you will live.'

But he wanted to justify himself, so he asked Jesus, 'And who is thy neighbour?'

In reply Jesus said: 'A man was going down from Jerusalem to Jericho, when he fell into the hands of robbers. They stripped him of his clothes, beat him and went away leaving him half-dead. A priest happened to be going down the same road, and when he saw the man, he passed by on the other side. So too, a Levite, when he came to the place and saw him, passed by on the other side. But a Samaritan, as he travelled, came where the man was; and when he saw him, took pity on him. He went to him and bandaged his wounds, pouring on oil and wine. Then he put the man on his own donkey, brought him to an inn and took

care of him. The next day he took out two silver coins and gave them to the innkeeper.

"Look after him," he said "and when I return, I will reimburse you for any extra expense you may have."

'Which of these three do you think was a neighbour to the man who fell into the hands of robbers?'

The expert in the law replied, 'The one who had mercy on him.'

Jesus told him, 'Go and do likewise.'

Jesus told this story in response to the question 'Who is thy neighbour?' As the story developed listeners would have changed their attitude.

When the priest came along they expected him to help. But he walked on. The excuse might have been he would have become technically unclean if he touched the man, then would not be allowed to work in the temple again for a month.

The crowd would have expected the Levite to help. They were godly helpers in the temple. His excuse might have been he would be late for temple duties or the same as the priest.

When the Samaritan came along, the crowd expected murder! You can imagine the gasps as he helps the man, takes him to an inn and then pays for the week. Who is thy neighbour? Anyone who is in need, regardless of race, colour, religion – even your enemy!

Galatians 3: 28 (All one in Christ)

There is neither Jew nor Greek, slave nor free, male nor female, for you are all one in Christ Jesus.

Paul points out that in God's eyes we are all equal. Some people say that this passage is against slavery – but it does not say that. However, it does say that God does not put one person above the other. This links with other passages of Paul's, such as his idea of the Church as a body made up of different parts, Christ as the head and all the parts of equal importance.

Acts 11: 1–18 (Peter and Cornelius)

The **apostles** and brothers throughout Judea heard that the Gentiles also had received the word of God. So when Peter went up to Jerusalem, the circumcized believers criticized him and said, 'You went into the house of uncircumcized men and ate with them.'

Peter began and explained everything to them precisely as it had happened: 'I was in the city of Joppa praying, and in a trance I saw a vision. I saw something like a large sheet being let down from heaven by its four corners, and it came down to where I was. I looked into it and saw four-footed animals of the earth, wild beasts, reptiles, and birds of the air. Then I heard a voice telling me, "Get up, Peter. Kill and eat."

'I replied, "Surely not, Lord! Nothing impure or unclean has ever entered my mouth."

'The voice spoke from heaven a second time, "Do not call anything impure that God has made clean." This happened three times, and then it was pulled up to heaven again.

'Right then three men who had been sent to me from Caesarea stopped at the house where I was staying. The Spirit told me to have no hesitation about going with them.

These six brothers also went with me, and we entered the man's house. He told us how he had seen an angel appear in his house and say, "Send to Joppa for Simon who is called Peter. He will bring you a message through which you and all your household will be saved."

'As I began to speak, the Holy Spirit came on them as he had come on us at the beginning. Then I remembered what the Lord had said: "John baptized with water, but you will be baptized with the Holy Spirit." So if God gave them the same gift as he gave us, who believed in the Lord Jesus Christ, who was I to think that I could oppose God?'

When they heard this, they had no further objections and praised God, saying, 'So then, God has granted even the Gentiles repentance unto life.'

Peter's prejudices were challenged by God. Peter dreamt about Jewish food laws – **kosher** and non-kosher food all mixed up together. Peter was horrified. On three occasions Peter was told to eat. God said that he had made everything and made them clean. Peter woke and men sent by Cornelius arrived.

Peter later explained that if he had not had the dream, he probably would not have gone. Peter would not have thought the gospel was for gentiles on the whole. But this clearly showed Peter that the gospel is for gentiles too, and God has made them clean. No longer would these rituals keep people from knowing about God's kingdom.

Activity

What can Christians learn about dealing with people of other races or religions from the parable of the Good Samaritan? Make a list. **PS 2.1, 2.2**

Set passages (cont.)

Luke 7: 1–10
(The centurion's servant)

When Jesus had finished saying all this in the hearing of the people, he entered Capernaum. There a centurion's servant, whom his master valued highly, was sick and about to die. The centurion heard of Jesus and sent some elders of the Jews to him, asking him to come and heal his servant. When they came to Jesus, they pleaded earnestly with him, 'This man deserves to have you do this, because he loves our nation and has built our synagogue.' So Jesus went with them.

He was not far from the house when the centurion sent friends to say to him: 'Lord, don't trouble yourself, for I do not deserve to have you come under my roof. This why I did not even consider myself worthy to come to you. But say the word, and my servant will be healed. For I myself am a man under authority, with soldiers under me. I tell this one, "Go," and he goes; and that one, "Come," and he comes. I say to my servant, "Do this," and he does it.'

When Jesus heard this, he was amazed at him, and turning to the crowd following him, he said, 'I tell you, I have not found such great faith even in Israel.' Then the men who had been sent returned to the house and found the servant well.

The centurion was Roman. This did not matter to Jesus, but the centurion showed respect for Judaism. He recognized in Jesus an authoritative person and said if he issued a command it would be done. He saw in Jesus someone who was greater than he. Jesus healed the servant.

The key phrase here is 'I tell you, I have not found such great faith even in Israel!'

Notice, too, we are not told if the servant was Jewish or not. We are not told anything about the servant's origins at all.

What is important is that the centurion showed great faith and believed Jesus could help his servant. He also showed respect for another person's religion and had found out some of the important customs. Additionally, he saw in Jesus a person superior to himself.

Other relevant passages

Deuteronomy 24: 14–15, 17, 19, 21–22

Do not take advantage of a hired man who is poor and needy, whether he is a brother Israelite or an alien [foreigner] living in one of your towns. Pay him his wages each day before sunset, because he is poor and counting on it … (14–15)

Do not deprive the alien or the fatherless of justice, or take the cloak of the widow as a pledge. (17)

When you are harvesting in your field and you overlook a sheaf, do not go back to get it. Leave it for the alien, the fatherless and the widow, so that the Lord your God may bless you in all the work of your hands. (19)

When you harvest the grapes in your vineyard, do not go over the vines again. Leave what remains for the alien, the fatherless and the widow. Remember that you were slaves in Egypt. That is why I command you to do this. (21–22)

God gives the Hebrew people strict instructions about the care of foreigners (some translations say 'aliens'). When the harvest is over, the poor and the foreigners are to be allowed to gather the leftovers. Wages, too, should be paid on time. God reminds his people of the time when they were persecuted in Egypt.

James 2: 1–9

My brothers, as believers in our glorious Lord Jesus Christ, don't show favouritism. Suppose a man comes into your meeting wearing a gold ring and fine clothes, and a poor man in shabby clothes also comes in. If you show special attention to the man wearing fine clothes and say, 'Here's a good seat for you,' but say to the poor man, 'You stand there' or 'Sit on the floor by my feet,' have you not discriminated among yourselves and become judges with evil thoughts?'

Listen, my dear brothers: Has not God chosen those who are poor in the eyes of the world to be rich in faith and to inherit the kingdom he promised to those who love him? But you have insulted the poor. Is it not the rich who are exploiting you? Are they not the ones who are dragging you into court? Are they not the ones who are slandering the noble name of him to whom you belong?

If you really keep the royal law found in Scripture, 'Love your neighbour as yourself,' you are doing right. But if you show favouritism, you sin and are convicted by the law as law-breakers.

This passage is often too true for comfort. The rich visitor is given priority over the poor, shabbily dressed visitor to church. James explains that God hates this. It is often the rich who exploit the poor and make them poorer. Treating someone differently because they are rich or poor, or by their looks, is just as much a **sin** as anything else.

Activities

1   Briefly outline and explain one Bible passage that a Christian could use to support the view that prejudice and discrimination are wrong. **C 2.2**

2   Why does James make favouritism such a wrong thing to do? What in fact could this lead to? Give reasons. **C 2.2, PS 2.1**

Exam questions to practise

Below are some sample exam questions for paper 2A. To help you score full marks, the first two questions are followed by some tips from examiners. Before attempting the remaining two questions, try to work out your own strategy for approaching them.

1 Explain how prejudice leads to discrimination. (3)

2 **a** Name a Christian who has worked to get rid of prejudice and discrimination. (1)

   b Describe how this Christian went about his or her work, including some successes and failures. (5)

   c What made this Christian do what he or she did? (3)
   (based on AQA 2002)

Now try questions 3 and 4 on your own. Before you write your answers, spend some time thinking about your approach.

3 What can we learn from Jesus about our attitudes towards:
   a people of a different race
   b people who are disabled? (4)

4 'Getting rid of prejudice will create world peace.' Do you agree? Give reasons for your answer, showing you have thought about more than one point of view. Refer to Christianity. (5)

How to do well

1 First define 'prejudice' and 'discrimination'. Then show how one leads to the other. Give some examples.

2 **a** Make sure the person you name is a Christian. Gandhi was not a Christian and you would get no marks for his name. You only need to write the person's name – nothing else.

   b Do not write the person's life history! Only write about his or her aims and good works. You should give a reasonably full answer.

   c Here you are writing about what motivated or inspired this Christian to do what he or she did. Give suitable quotes, for example from the Bible, that are relevant.

Christian responsibility: aid for developing countries

'Poverty? What poverty? There's no such thing in Britain!'
'Poverty belongs to poor countries in Africa and South America.'
'If you're poor in Britain it's your own fault.'

Many people believe these things. In this section we will discuss poverty in Britain and in developing countries. There is information about four leading Christian voluntary agencies. We read about Oscar Romero, who died serving the poor. Bible passages reveal what Jesus said about wealth and how it should be used.

This section includes:

- A divided world
- Debt
- Child six billion
- Population
- Education
- Diseases and health care
- Short and long-term aid
- Tearfund and CAFOD
- Christian Aid and Trócaire
- Raising awareness in the UK
- Oscar Romero
- The rich/poor divide in the UK
- Poverty in the UK
- Bible passages 1
- Bible passages 2
- Exam questions to practise

A divided world

Key terms

Malnutrition The effects of not having a balanced diet.

Poverty cycle People are poor, cannot afford education, so have low-paid, unskilled jobs. They cannot escape from poverty.

Developing country Poor country that is developing better economic or social conditions. (Used to be known as a third world country.)

The resources in the world are not equally shared out. In many areas the rich are getting richer and the poor are getting poorer.

Enough to go round?

About 20 per cent of the world's population have 80 per cent of the resources!

Differences between the rich world and poor world

Rich world	Poor world
FOOD	
Plenty of food and varied diet.	Very little food, limited diet.
Food is wasted.	Malnutrition common, and diseases – for example, rickets.
Obesity is a growing problem.	
WATER	
Clean water 'on tap'.	Most water contaminated.
Each house has running water.	A well in a village is a luxury.
Separate sanitation and fresh water system.	Sewage mixes with drinking water.
EDUCATION	
In the UK, education from age four to eighteen is free.	Many have no free schooling.
Choice of private schooling.	Rely on donations for school.
All children must go to school or good home tuition must be provided.	Little chance of education for poor children.
HEALTH	
In the UK medical care is free.	No free treatment.
Choice of private or **NHS**.	No choice.
Most people live near a hospital.	Nearest hospital up to 300 miles away.
Plenty of doctors available.	Doctors may do clinics only every three months.
Latest in medical care.	Outdated technology and medicines.
HOUSING	
Housing is generally good.	Shelter built from what materials can be found.
Houses have water, gas, toilet and electricity.	

Five basic needs

Human beings have five basic needs:

food, water, health, education, work.

Most countries would agree, but some say that their country cannot afford to do anything about it.

- *Food*. This is essential for life. Without it the body will die. If you do not receive a regular, balanced diet you will suffer from **malnutrition**. You have no energy, you cannot work, so you earn no money.

- *Water*. This keeps the body alive. Dirty water is a potential killer. Dirty water can cause many illnesses. River blindness is caused by a parasite that gets in the eyes when washing. Cholera is spread rapidly by dirty water and is highly **contagious** (catching).

- *Health*. It is better to prevent **disease** than to have to cure it. So children are **vaccinated** against diseases like measles, polio and tuberculosis (TB). In poor countries there is a shortage of trained staff, medicines and X-ray machines.

- *Education*. Basic education should be free and available to all children. Poor countries cannot afford to feed their people, so education is a luxury. With education,

children can begin to leave the **poverty cycle**. It helps them to get a skilled job. Many people in the UK sponsor a child's education by giving a monthly donation.

- *Work*. Even in the UK, during times of high unemployment people have talked about 'their right to a job', or the country 'owing it to them'. In most **developing countries** if you do not work, you do not eat.

Activities

Get into groups of four.
a Work out a list of five things you could not do without in your lives. (You can assume that you will have food and water, so you do not need to count these in your list.)
b Do you think a very poor child in India would have chosen anything you did? Give reasons. Discuss in your groups or as a class. C 2.1a, WO 2.1, 2.3

Key points

- There are many differences between rich and poor countries.

- What people in the UK would call a 'basic necessity' might be a luxury in a developing country.

Debt

Many developing countries have huge **debts**. The amount they owe increases weekly as the interest grows. Trying to pay off the debt is a serious problem for the countries concerned. For example, sub-Saharan Africa pays back US$10 billion every year from a loan. This is four times as much money as the region spends each year on health and education.

Loans and debts

At the end of the 1970s, oil-exporting countries such as the USA had much wealth. The banks loaned the money to developing countries at low interest rates. The money should have been used to build schools, and set up health systems and other schemes. Often, corrupt government officials spent it on themselves or bought weapons.

The interest rates began to rise. Developing countries began to earn less as prices of export food fell.

Developing countries now owe money to Western banks, the International Monetary Fund (IMF) and even their own banks. In December 2000, 41 countries were said to be heavily in debt. Their debt now stands at US$215 billion. In 1980, this debt was only US$55 billion.

The poorest people lose out. Fertile land is used to grow crops for export only. Farmers starve while food such as coffee is shipped out to other countries.

FACT In 1994, Africa's debt was £5 billion. This has now almost trebled. In 1994, people in the UK spent £5 billion on sweets, chocolate and crisps!

The debt grows!

Loans have to be paid off in hard currency (for example, the UK pound, the US dollar, the Japanese yen). If the value of a developing country's money goes down, the debt rises as it takes more of the developing country's money to buy the hard currency.

Solution

A simple solution would be to cancel the debts. The original loans have been repaid many times over, in interest.

FACT The total cost of wiping out the debt of the twenty worst affected countries would be between £3.5 billion and £4.54 billion. This is what it cost to build Euro Disney.

DROP THE DEBT NOW!

Progress is greatest when ordinary people are demanding political, economic and social change.

Jubilee 2000 Coalition – end the debt!

Several voluntary agencies, mostly Christian, joined together to call for the end of third world debt.

Church on the Hill

PETITION

1. We, the undersigned believe that the start of the new millennium should be a time to give hope to the impoverished countries of the world.

2. To make a fresh start we believe it right to put behind us the mistakes made by leaders and borrowers and to cancel the backlog of unpayable debts of the most Impoverished Nations.

3. We call upon the leaders of lending nations to write off these debts by the year 2000. We also ask them to take steps to prevent such high levels of debt building up again.

Sign below if you support the Petition

Name _____

Email _____

City _____

Country _____

Tearfund sold badges made to look like a link chain with the slogan 'Break the chains of debt campaign'.

There were rallies in the UK and in many other countries during the year 2000. Jubilee 2000 groups joined worldwide in a human chain in 600 events, where people linked arms and held candles.

Many celebrities gave their backing. Over 300,000 emails were sent to **G8** delegates when they met in Okinawa in July 2000. One website, 'Drop the Debt', provided news updates.

The UK Chancellor of the Exchequer, Gordon Brown, announced in July 2000 that some countries would have their debts to the UK cancelled. Welcome news, but the campaign goes on.

Activity

Who is to blame for the debts owed by developing countries? Discuss this in a class debate to get some ideas. Then use these ideas to act out a role-play. You will need eight people.

Four representatives (banker, politician, trader and farmer) from developing countries meet four representatives (banker, politician, trader and Jubilee 2000 campaigner) from a Western country – the UK. The representatives sit around a table to work out who or what is to blame for the debt. **C 2.1a, 2.1b, WO 2.2**

Key points

- Debt is an increasing problem.
- Paying back interest diverts money from where it is needed.

There are now more than six billion humans on earth today. In fact, child six billion was born sometime between June and October 1999. By 2015 it is estimated that there will be seven billion people. By 2050, low estimates suggest ten billion people.

Is the earth too crowded?

The world's population has grown since Victorian times. In 1960, there were three billion people. By 2000 there were over six billion people.

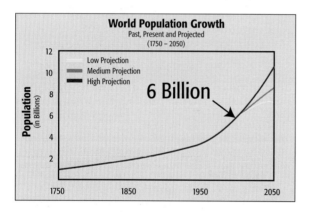

A billion is a thousand million: 1,000,000,000.

Why did the population rise so quickly?

In the developed world couples are having fewer children. But in other societies it is usual to have large families. Now, more children are surviving until their sixteenth birthdays. Then they have their own children.

Problems and solutions

- *Problems.* The rise in population has caused problems. Everyone needs the same basic necessities to live – for example, food, water, shelter, health care. Food and water are becoming scarce as more people use them. Humans are using up natural resources.

- *Solutions.* One solution is to ensure everyone has access to family planning. The next is to handle the world with care to preserve its natural resources.

The world of child six billion

Child six billion may well have been born in your local maternity unit! What sort of world was it born into? Take another look at pages 8–11 of this book.

- *Child six billion will grow up in a world concerned about air.* Air pollutants cause ill-health, especially heart and lung disease. They also cause global warming and create acid rain. Forests and vegetation can be part of the solution. Governments now realize the importance of forests and try to protect them.

- *Child six billion will grow up in a world concerned about water.* A picture from the air shows a world covered in water. But most of it is salt, sea-water. About 70 per cent of the fresh water is frozen – the polar ice-caps and glaciers. Fresh water for drinking and industry is very limited.

From space, the world appears to be covered in water.

Agencies such as Oxfam and CAFOD are working on water catchment projects in the developing world. This means digging out large hollows in the land to catch water when it rains. This is then used to water trees to provide fuel and food.

● *Child six billion will grow up in a world concerned about nutrition.* People in rich countries eat too much, yet there are millions of children with vitamin deficiency diseases.

> **FACT** More than 800 million people do not have enough to eat, and millions are starving.
>
> **FACT** More than one-third of under-fives in the world are underweight.
>
> **FACT** One child under five will die from hunger (or illness) every 2.7 seconds. How many will die during your lesson?

● *Child six billion will grow up in a world concerned about health* (see pages 120–121). In less than one minute (time it), one child under five will have died from one of the five preventable diseases: pneumonia, diarrhoea, measles, malaria and malnutrition. Malaria is spread by mosquitoes. Local villagers get help to get rid of stagnant water areas, the breeding ground for mosquitoes.

> **FACT** Malaria kills over twice as many people as AIDS.
>
> **FACT** Malaria is the second largest cause of illness in the world.

● *Child six billion will grow up in a world concerned about housing.* Even in the UK there are homeless people. Habitat for Humanity works with the homeless in many countries. Habitat for Humanity has built 300,000 homes in 59 countries.

Should people have to live in homes like this?

● *Child six billion will grow up in a world concerned about education* (see pages 118–119). In the poorest countries only 62 per cent of men and 38 per cent of women can read. Education is needed to help people escape the poverty cycle and to promote equality.

Activities

1 Describe in your own words the world into which child six billion was born. **C 2.2**

2 Write a poem about the kind of world you would like your children to grow up in. **C 2.3**

Key points

● Child six billion was born into a world where people have identified the main problems.

● There are solutions, but they cannot happen overnight.

Most populated countries

1	China	1.237 billion
2	India	1.014 billion
3	USA	275 million
4	Indonesia	224 million
5	Brazil	172 million
6	Russia	146 million
7	Pakistan	141 million
8	Bangladesh	129 million
9	Japan	126 million
10	Nigeria	123 million
20	UK	59 million

Most populated cities

1	Tokyo (Japan)	34.8 million
2	New York (USA)	20.2 million
3	Seoul (S Korea)	19.9 million
4	Mexico City (Mexico)	19.8 million
5	Sao Paulo (Brazil)	17.9 million
6	Mumbai (formerly Bombay, India)	17.8 million
7	Osaka (Japan)	17.7 million
8	Los Angeles (USA)	16.2 million
9	Cairo (Egypt)	14.4 million
10	Manila (Philippines)	13.5 million
17	London (UK)	11.8 million

Why are people attracted to big cities?

Yes, population growth is slowing down, but 80 million babies are born each year. Even the lowest estimate says there will be 10 billion people by 2050. There will still be 2 billion people short of clean water by 2050.

Myths about population

Myth 1

Rapid population growth is not much of a problem now. What will be the effect of the world's population going down?

Myth 2

If the population does grow, humans are clever enough to invent new technology to help.

The earth's natural resources (such as coal and oil) will run out. There is no way of replacing these resources.

Myth 3

Hunger and famine have been caused by too many people living in one place.

Yes, some areas have famine because the local people cannot grow enough of a good range of healthy food. But famine and hunger are also caused by farmers not being paid a fair price for their goods/food.

Myth 4

Population growth in poor countries means the people will always be poor.

Children in large families receive less education than those in smaller families. Education is the escape route for leaving the poverty trap for many people.

Myth 5

You cannot impose family planning on people who do not want it.

As part of a general health care service for developing countries, aid agencies provide:

- free contraceptives, and teach about planned parenthood

- health care for pregnant women

- training for local women to be midwives

- post-natal care and encouraging breast-feeding (this helps to reduce the number of babies/children who die)

- health care for all women, especially those who have had many children

- education about how to avoid **HIV**/AIDS and other diseases.

Myth 6

The UK spends too much sending aid to poor countries.

In 1994, many countries met to discuss population. Increased grants have meant more midwife training and education about family planning and the prevention of diseases. The developing countries agreed to pay some of the costs. The UK, France, Denmark and Germany give about two to three per cent of their budgets to foreign aid. The USA gives less than one per cent.

Activities

1 Find out what the current world population figures are. Have these figures grown much since child six billion in 1999? Work out the percentage rise. A good place to start your research is the US Census Bureau website which can be accessed via www.heinemann.co.uk/hotlinks. **IT 2.1**

2 Which world problem – debt or population – do you think is the most important? Give reasons. **PS 2.2**

Key points

- The world's population continues to grow rapidly.

- Some countries cannot provide enough food and clean water for their people.

- There are many myths about population growth.

Education

The Declaration of Human Rights says: 'Primary education should be free and compulsory for all.'

> **FACT** One-third of people in developing countries cannot read or write.
>
> **FACT** In 2000, 125 million children aged between six and eleven years had no schooling.
>
> **FACT** In 2000, a further 149 million children left school before they could read or write fluently.

The benefits of education

- *Why get educated?* Education helps you to get a job or to improve your skills. This can enable you to support your family and to help your country's economy.

- *Why are people with no education likely to be very poor?* Mainly because they are likely to be unemployed, or farming to grow food just for their family.

- *How does education help people to escape poverty?* If you gain new skills this can help you to grow more crops. For example, a farmer in Uganda with primary education could raise his output on the farm by seven per cent – the difference between life and death.

- *How can education save lives?* Every year millions of children die as a result of avoidable diseases. When children are educated, they can learn about health care. When they grow up they will know how to prevent disease and teach this to their children.

An example of making a difference

A nursery teacher went to Vietnam to see agencies working with the poorest children.

The teacher travelled to a remote area, Lao Cai, high in the mountains. The majority of its inhabitants are **ethnic minorities**. They have their own cultures, traditions and languages.

Families told their visitor that they now regard a basic education as essential. 'If you read you can follow instructions on fertilizers and equipment for farming.' 'You can read what it says about the medicine you are taking.' 'Basic numeracy means not being cheated on prices and weights.'

Community education

Community education is not just for children. It aims to teach whole communities about various issues – for example, AIDS awareness or a particular farming technique. It helps the community gain resources and to work out their future.

Voluntary agencies aim, where possible, to train local people, who then go out to the communities and teach. For example, community education in South Africa focuses on HIV/AIDS work in many areas.

Inequalities in Education

Public money. Rich countries spend a lot of government money on education. But in South Asia, which has a quarter of the world's population, the government spends only four per cent of its money on education. This works out at US$5,130 per primary school pupil in the USA and US$3,553 in the UK. In Nepal and India the government spend US$12 per child.

Personal spending. In richer countries families spend a great deal of money on books, CDs, music lessons, videos, computers, etc. In poor countries families cannot afford this. A recent survey found that 80 per cent of primary age children in the UK have more than 25 books at home.

Ways of helping

- *Supporting agencies.* Many Christians believe it is their duty to help those in need. They think education is very important. There are some agencies that concentrate on children (such as Save the Children), and others that have general education projects (such as CAFOD and VSO).

- *Sponsoring a child's education.* Some Christians choose to sponsor a child's education – a popular idea at the moment. There are many reasons for doing this, some of which will be personal (see below). People donate a monthly sum of money. The average at the moment is £12 per month. Some schools link with a school that is being supported, and each class will sponsor at least one pupil.

Sponsoring a child's education

- The person believes in the value of education.

- The person is a Christian who wishes to follow Jesus' example of teaching anyone who listened.

- Parents may sponsor a child as a family project. They teach their own children what they have to be thankful for.

Key points

- Many children receive little or no education.

- Education is one way to escape the poverty trap.

Diseases and health care

Key terms

Disease Illness that may cause early death, disfigurement or disability.

Vaccination Protects against disease by injecting with vaccine (to immunize).

Primary health care Prevention of illness.

In developing countries, every day, 13,500 children die of one of the five avoidable diseases: pneumonia, diarrhoea, malaria, measles and malnutrition. Dirty water also causes many diseases.

Primary health care

Primary health care aims to prevent disease before you get it.

```
                    Correct food advice
                            |
    Vaccinations                    Regular clinics/
              \                    /    surgeries
                 ( Primary )
                 ( health care )
              /                    \
    Trained                         Clean water
    midwives and                    in every
    health visitors                 village
                            |
            Regular checks on growth,
            weight and health of children
```

Management of childhood illness (IMCI)

The aid agencies that aim to improve child health agreed on a plan to give training on how to recognize and deal with the five main causes of child deaths. They printed out lists of symptoms and how to treat them. They gave out treatment kits that were real life-savers.

HIV/AIDS in Uganda

Uganda was one of the first African states to see the totally devastating effects of HIV/AIDS. The government worked with religious leaders, medics, voluntary agencies and tribal chiefs to reduce the rate each year.

- Sex education in schools taught about the spread of HIV.

- Radio broadcasts did the same as schools.

- Same-day testing and counselling clinics were set up.

> **FACT** In ten years more than 1.5 million children have become orphans in Uganda as a result of AIDS.

Vitamin A deficiency

A shortage of Vitamin A is the main cause of blindness in the world, and it is very common in India and Indonesia. It can be treated easily with Vitamin A tablets. But for a long-term solution a better diet and education is needed.

Why the lack of Vitamin A?

- People do not know about healthy diets. Vitamin A is found in fish oils, milk, eggs, carrots, chilli, papaya and green vegetables such as spinach. Others, who breast-feed their children until they are three or four years old, also lack Vitamin A and so pass this onto their children.

- Poor families can only afford rice and it is only on special occasions that they might add some vegetables.

The need for clean water

> **FACT** More than 600 people die every hour because they have no water or the little they have is dirty.

By 2025, two-thirds of the world's people will face water shortages. Some countries suffer because there is little rainfall, but for most the problem is lack of access to clean water.

> **FACT** One in four people in the developing world has no access to safe water.

In some developing countries, governments work with aid agencies to set up local projects. For example, Tearfund supported churches in Ethiopia with community-based water projects. It tested for clean water, drilled wells and set up pumps. The communities felt these were their projects. They had a sense of ownership.

> **FACT** When you next flush the loo, you will use more water than a Ugandan uses in a day.

Dehydration caused by diarrhoea

Poor sanitation and dirty water cause diarrhoea. In the year 2000, three million children died. About 80 per cent of these were aged under two. Many of them died from dehydration due to diarrhoea. This figure breaks down to:

- 8000 a day
- six every minute
- one every ten seconds.

If more than ten per cent of body fluid is lost, a person will die. There are several ways of preventing dehydration:

- setting up sanitation projects and digging wells
- educating mothers that breast feeding a baby will usually prevent diarrhoea
- vaccination of all children against illnesses such as typhoid, diphtheria and so on.

A DROP OF LUXURY

Everyone should be able to get their hands on clean water.

More than 600 people die every hour because they have no water, or because the little they have is dirty.

With your help Tearfund partners can reach more people with safe water, food, healthcare and other basic necessities. Luxuries they can't afford to be without.

Agencies work with local communities to provide clean water.

Activity

Imagine you are the Director of Health Projects for a Christian agency (for example, Tearfund or CAFOD). List, with reasons, your top five projects. You can do this as a group collaboration, later presenting your findings to the rest of the class. C 2.1b, WO 2.1, 2.2

Key points

- Primary health care is important. It is far better to prevent illness than to try to cure it.
- Many governments work closely with aid agencies to improve medical care.
- The focus of many projects is mother and baby care.

Short and long-term aid

Key terms

Aid Help sent to countries in need either in an emergency or over the long term.

Short-term aid Emergency aid sent because of a disaster like an earthquake.

Long-term aid Aid spread over many years with the goal of self-reliance to those receiving it.

Richer countries and voluntary agencies send **aid** to developing countries when a need occurs.

Short-term (emergency) aid

Aid agencies send help to an area affected by a disaster. Voluntary agencies send various sorts of **short-term aid**, such as:

- sniffer dogs and heat-seeking devices following an earthquake, to find survivors

- shelter, mainly in the form of tents, for refugees fleeing from **war** and for those who are homeless following a disaster

- medical aid at the start of a disaster to help with casualties; it is used to vaccinate children and adults against water-borne diseases such as cholera

- emergency clean-up facilities; this prevents the spread of disease, by burying dead people and animals

- basic food, such as rice and powdered milk, to help keep victims alive

- dehydration kits, to prevent death due to dehydration caused by diarrhoea

- landmine clearance teams to make an area safe before people return to their homes; they teach them how to seek out these mines and what to do.

An example: Venezuela

In the middle of 2000, Venezuela faced a huge disaster. It saw the heaviest rainfall ever recorded. Most of this rain fell in the most populated area in the north. The rain caused mud slides and flooding. Whole villages disappeared, as did roads and railways. Within two days, 30,000 people were dead.

The first stage of aid was to rescue survivors and bury the dead. The second stage was to supply tents, medicine and food. The donation of clothes was a success. Aid workers wrote out lists of medical supplies needed in the short term and the long term. Many drugs companies donated essentials such as antibiotics. Long-term aid will bring the rebuilding of roads and new towns, and prevention of disease.

UK specialist teams work to find earthquake victims in India.

Long-term aid

This type of aid may have to go on for many years. The aim is to enable the country to manage on its own, and its people to make their own decisions.

Christian voluntary agencies work with local churches. The churches know the area, the language, local customs and where help is most needed.

Here is a list of some **long-term aid** that agencies give to countries in need.

- They give tools and basic equipment to farmers, and teach them modern farming methods. They may establish 'model farms' where people can come and see the methods in action.

- Medical aid is needed all the time. This could be a vaccination programme or setting up a clinic. The main aim is to prevent illness through primary health care.

- Building materials and help so people can build good quality homes. For example, homes must withstand earthquakes.

- Tearfund has a project to knock down **shanty towns** in India and rebuild with brick or stone and with sanitation. Local people are then taught how to maintain the systems.

- Education is for everyone. This includes health education and care for the environment.

- Voluntary agencies provide training in skills such as farming, midwifery, nursing, building, sewing and road building. This helps people to do things for themselves.

- Fair Trade and Tradecraft. In this project, buyers pay a fair price for produce or goods from developing countries. For example, Café Direct ensures that coffee and tea producers receive a fair wage.

An example: Hunger project works in Peru

It is not just Africa and India that have problems. The Hunger Project in Peru works with Peruvian groups that are committed to ending hunger and poverty.

The first project was in the Yurinaki River area. Local governments, community leaders and universities worked together. Five communities began the project. Priorities were to increase income and grow nutritional food. Farmers began to rebuild dilapidated coffee plantations. They tested and prepared soil. They built coffee plant hot houses to bring on coffee seedlings. Families began to grow food in their gardens and keep chickens. As a result, adults and children became healthier because they ate the right food. Surplus money was put back into the schemes. They grew new produce and set up a business making jewellery.

Activities

1 List the aid that you think Venezuela needs:
   a in the short term
   b in the long term. **PS 2.1**

2 Do you think it is right for rich countries to give aid to poor countries? List your reasons. **PS 2.1**

Key points

- Agencies in the UK support projects in a developing country working with groups like the local church.

- Many Christians see the exchange of ideas as the way forward.

Tearfund and CAFOD

Tearfund

Tearfund is a Christian relief agency. It aims to bring 'hope and help' to communities. In 2000, Tearfund supported 550 projects in 100 countries.

Tearfund works as a partner with other Christian groups and local churches. It helps people in need, regardless of their religion. But it is a Christian group, and puts God's love into action.

Tearfund works in health care and many other areas. It has a trading company, Tearcraft, that sells craft goods at fair prices.

Mission statement

The purpose of Tearfund is to serve Jesus Christ by enabling those who share evangelical Christian beliefs to bring good news to the poor.

If you give money to Tearfund, it can go into the general fund or you can ask for the money to go towards a special project. You can 'Become a Changemaker'.

There are five special projects, including *The Children at Risk* project. This new project helps abused children – for example, children who work eighteen hours a day, who are ill-treated or who are sexually abused. Many have seen their parents die in war.

A true story

Thouen lived in Cambodia. When she was fifteen years old she was sold for sex. She worked in a brothel for over two years, where the main clients were tourists. She was rescued by a local vicar and now lives in the House of Hope sponsored by Tearfund. Trained therapists and counsellors, plus many other people, are helping Thouen through her trauma.

CAFOD

CAFOD stands for Catholic Fund for Overseas Development. It supports over 500 projects in 75 countries. Recent projects include Landmines Action.

Mission statement

CAFOD aims to provide human development and social justice in witness to Christian faith and **Gospel** *values. Funds raised will: empower people to bring about change; raise public awareness about poverty and injustice; act for the poor; and challenge governments and international bodies to adopt policies with social justice.*

CAFOD, like Tearfund, is a partnership organization. This means it helps in times of emergency *and* it works with local people to help them overcome their problems long term. It never simply gives money.

CAFOD does all types of work. Examples include:

- rural work in Burkina Faso
- food and nutrition in Sudan
- human rights in Peru
- income projects in Cambodia
- disarming child soldiers in Sierra Leone.

Child soldiers

Sierra Leone is one country of many that uses child soldiers. It is usually rebel militia who force children to join – boys and girls, some as young as six. The militia often brand the children to show who is their leader.

CAFOD supports local leaders who are trying to set children free. Once rescued, the children receive help to get back into the community.

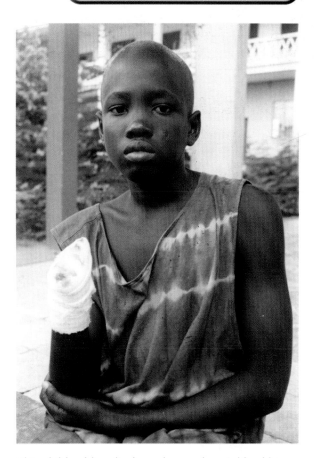

This child soldier disobeyed an order and had his hand chopped off as punishment.

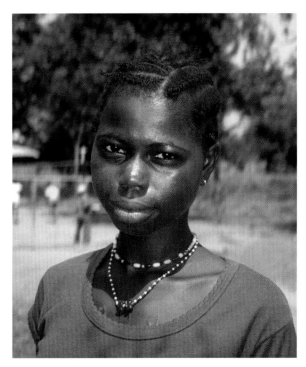

This child soldier was constantly raped and was branded with her General's initials using hot irons.

Activity

Why do you think Tearfund and CAFOD rely mainly on church donations? Do you think this is right? Give reasons. **C 2.1a**

Key points

- Tearfund and CAFOD rely mainly on donations from churches and support projects in developing countries often run by local churches.
- They bring the gospel of hope to the poor.
- The 1990s saw a new mood of cooperation, which avoided duplication of work.

Christian Aid

Christian ii Aid

We believe in life before death

Christian Aid works in some of the world's poorest communities in more than 50 countries. Christian Aid is supported by churches.

Christian Aid director Daleep Mukarji says: 'Our strength, identity and heritage – our niche – is that we are an agency of the churches, owned by the churches, helping churches work for a better world.'

Christian Aid, however, isn't just for Christians. It works where the need is greatest, helping people to tackle their problems whatever they believe. Aid is distributed on the basis of need not religion, race, creed or nationality.

Christian Aid is not a missionary organisation; it tries to live out its faith in practice. Its Christian values translate into an organisation that is bold in its message and purpose.

'I'm convinced that many who support us are not committed Christians, perhaps not Christians at all,' says Daleep Mukarji. 'But they recognise our values and commitment to justice and our track record, and find in Christian Aid a link from faith to meaningful action.'

In 2003–4 Christian Aid spent more than £60 million on development programmes and disaster relief. Christian Aid's work includes:

- helping farmers who once had nothing, giving them tools and seeds rather than money so that they can build a future

- fighting for rights for women who had no say

- working to build peace in communities torn apart by war

These Ethiopian refugees do not even have the luxury of a refugee camp.

- helping provide emergency provisions to those made homeless by natural disasters

- helping people with HIV get the medicine they need to help them raise their children.

An example: Sudan

At least two million people have been killed and four million forced to leave their homes during Sudan's civil war, which has lasted more than 20 years. The main conflict is between the Sudanese government based in the north and rebel groups in the south. However, peace talks are expected to result in an agreement by the summer of 2004.

Recent fighting in Darfur, western Sudan, however, threatens this peace deal. The fighting in Dafur needed an urgent disaster response. Christian Aid has contributed £50,000 through the Action by Churches Together appeal to help provide blankets, seeds and tools, basic healthcare, and emergency schooling to people affected by the conflict.

There are also many local conflicts between different religious and ethnic groups within southern Sudan. In the long-term, as part of peace agreements, Christian Aid and the New Sudan Council of Churches have implemented projects to promote peace, such as a primary school that will help children from different communities in southern Sudan to share an education and become friends.

A number of similar peacebuilding conferences have taken place in the south, helping to improve relationships between ethnic communities.

Christian Aid responds quickly when there is an emergency to provide immediate disaster relief. It is also there long-term, giving people a chance to live life to the full.

Trócaire

> ### Mission statement
>
> *We believe that it is only by changing the structures that perpetuate poverty and injustice, that we can have a real impact on the lives of the poor.*

Trócaire is the Irish Catholic agency for overseas development. Over the past 31 years, Trócaire has funded and/or implemented more than 8000 programmes in 60 countries worldwide.

At home, Trócaire raises awareness of the causes of poverty and injustice and organises campaigns to bring about global change.

Fair play for toy workers

This project began in 2000. It aimed to make the public aware of 'sweat shops', mainly in Asia, making cheap toys for Europe and the USA.

Fair Play for Toy Workers

New projects

Trócaire has just launched the Keep Our Word campaign which looks at the UN Millennium Development Goals, a set of 8 development targets. They aim to eradicate hunger and poverty, and to improve the lives of billions around the world.

Activities

1   Borrow or hire a video from one of the agencies and watch its work in action.
    C 1.2, WO 1.1, 2.2

2   **a**   Choose at least two of the following agencies:
    - Christian Aid
    - Trócaire
    - Tearfund
    - CAFOD.

    b   Divide a sheet of paper into two vertical columns and list the similarities and differences between the two chosen agencies.
    PS 2.2, 2.3

Key points

- Christian Aid and Trócaire share the aim of helping the poor and bringing the gospel of hope.

- As with Tearfund and CAFOD, these agencies are Christian, but will help anyone in need regardless of religion, race, gender, colour or disability.

- They are partnership agencies – they work with local communities, groups and churches, and fund their schemes.

Raising awareness in the UK

Voluntary agencies need donations to carry out their work. Churches support some (for example, CAFOD), while the public support others (for example, Oxfam). They prefer not to get money from the government. This allows them to be free from political control. Each agency has to make the public aware of its work and the needs of the poorest people.

Fund-raising

Christian voluntary agencies such as Tearfund and CAFOD get their funding mainly from churches. (This includes church groups such as youth groups.) Their schools' representatives are employed to visit and speak to groups to give up-to-date information.

Christian Aid is the UK's best known Christian agency. In May each year, there is Christian Aid Week and door-to-door collections.

Charity shops

There are many national charity shops, such as Oxfam, Help the Aged and Cancer Research. Local charity shops include Claire House Hospice and Nightingale Hospice. Charity shops follow a code of conduct – some of this code can be seen on this page.

Media

The **media** includes television, radio, video and newspapers.

- *The news*. Television news reports focus on tragedies or disasters. Agencies say that once the reports end so does general interest.

LOOK OUT!
FOR THIS NEW LOGO

making the most of your donations

Association of Charity Shops

Charities using this logo are making the most of your donations

Because they

- Run charity shops
- Use your donations to raise as much money as possible for their charities
- Meet their statutory obligations and operate under a code of good practice
- Are registered charities (or their trading companies)

Look out for this logo in charity shops on house to house collection sacks on clothing/book banks

This logo will be on display in many shops as a symbol of quality assurance.

- *Videos*. Agencies use professional video-makers so that their work can be shown. Many videos are aimed at a certain age group – for example, Tear Tots for Key Stage 1.

- *Resources*. These are for different age groups – for example, Tearfund Activ 1st is four fourteen to sixteen year-olds, with a regular magazine and posters. It deals with real people in real countries and cities.

Using famous people

Most agencies try to involve someone well known, perhaps as a patron. For example, Princess Diana was patron of the Leprosy Mission. Sometimes these patrons are active supporters. For example, Princess Anne, the Princess Royal, is patron of Save the Children Fund. She goes on well-publicized visits to projects abroad.

Some famous people may become involved with a one-off cause. For example, Robbie Williams has visited various projects in Africa on behalf of Comic Relief.

The use of someone famous or royalty can be beneficial. Some people will give saying, 'If this is supported by X then it must be OK.' When Princess Diana was filmed and photographed hugging and holding hands with AIDS patients, she did more good than hours of telling people 'It is safe to touch someone with AIDS'.

Posters

People say that posters are a life line for agencies. They need a good picture and catchy slogan. Voluntary agencies also need professional advertising or they would lose money.

Christian Aid chose the slogan 'We believe in life *before* death'. When it appeared on a picture of a water pump, it showed that something very simple can keep people alive.

Some posters aim to shock. Others show before-and-after pictures. Here are some slogans.

- Children are the heart of our future!

- The greatest natural resource a country can have is its children!

- GOD@work!

- Could you feed your family with a handful of seeds?

Activities

1 Look back at the text on posters and slogans.
   a Think carefully about each slogan. Make a note about whether each slogan appeals to you or not.
   b Either describe or draw what you think the picture would be for these slogans.
   c Share your ideas with a partner or a group. **C 2.3, WO 2.2**

2 Draw or paint the final poster. **IT 2.3**

Key points

- A voluntary agency relies on donations to carry out its work.

- Campaigning has to be done well or the charity will lose out.

- The media generally highlight the bad things going on in the world, but their interest does not last.

Oscar Romero (1917–1980)

'I must tell you, as a Christian, I do not believe in death without resurrection. If I am killed I shall arise in the people of El Salvador.'

1917	Born in El Salvador. Trained as a priest, then further studies in Rome. Worked as priest in many parishes in El Salvador.
1977	Became Archbishop of San Salvador. Used his position to speak out against the corrupt government and against the death squads. Supported the poor people who were getting poorer. Called himself a pastor, ready to give his life for his flock. Received death threats - challenged death squads to a debate.
March 1980	Murdered as he **consecrated** the bread and wine in the **Mass**.
Other details	He urged peaceful reform, asking God to overcome the spirit of hatred and revenge. He was prepared to give the new government a chance to reform.

What made Romero do what he did?

Christians serve others but St Paul says 'Obey your government'.

So what happens if a country is ruled by a **dictator** backed by the army? What if the government is corrupt, evil and anti-Christian?

Romero studied hard. He found the rich got richer, the poor got poorer and opponents of the government disappeared. He decided that 'if the church serves God, then Christians will come into conflict with (South American) governments'.

Liberation theology

God is a liberator – he sets people free. God supports poor people and is involved in politics!

Archbishop Romero of San Salvador

Romero kept paperwork as low as possible and looked after his people. He campaigned for peace, for enough food and medical care. At Mass, Romero always preached on his themes of peace, justice and ending corruption.

Attacks

Many priests were murdered, as were leaders of the poor. The government was unhappy about Romero – people were coming to the cathedral to hear uncensored news.

Threats

Despite threats, Romero still walked the streets and told the world's journalists what was happening. Romero knew he could not keep quiet, even though government death squads hanged hundreds of people and left them hanging with warnings carved into their bodies. He wrote to the US President saying, 'Please do not send any more weapons to El Salvador!'

Premonition

Romero felt he would die soon. On a visit to Rome he prayed for courage to die in faith.

New life: 24 March 1980

Romero was shot as he celebrated the Mass in his Cathedral. In his sermon, he had preached about a seed in the ground which had to die in order to give new life.

Martyrdom

Today, people in El Salvador think Romero is a **martyr**.

Instead of one person, three people offered to do his work. When they were murdered, then four more carried on his work. Romero was, indeed, like the seed that dies in order to grow and multiply.

Activities

1 Discuss the following questions in groups, then write down your answers.
   a Do you think that Romero was foolish to get in conflict with the government?
   b Do you think Romero achieved anything?
   c If yes, then what?
   d Do you think Christians today should get involved in politics?
   e Are there any issues that you think Christians should/should not get involved in? C 2.1a, WO 2.1, 2.3

2 Do you think Romero should be made a saint? List your reasons. PS 2.1

Key points

- Liberation **theology** is the idea that the gospel is one of hope for the poor that will inevitably lead to clashes between church and state.

- It is based on Jesus' words in Luke 4: 18, 'The spirit of the Lord is upon me.'

- Some people still believe that Romero stirred up trouble. Romero said he was a shepherd of his flock, prepared to die for them, as he did not feel that he could remain silent.

The UK in 2001: the rich/poor divide.

There is an idea in some British minds that if a family is poor, it is all their own fault. In the 1970s, 'north-south divide' became a political term. Basically it means there is an imaginary line drawn across Britain from the west to the east with areas south of the line being rich and those in the north being poor. The divide is often described as:

- the 'haves' and the 'have nots'
- the employed and the unemployed
- skilled workers and unskilled workers

- those with a private pension and those who rely on the state pension
- those who can manage their money and those who cannot
- those who save and those who do not.

Characteristics

Research groups have drawn up a list of characteristics found in many poor regions.

- High unemployment – 3.7 per cent in south-east versus 10.1 per cent in the north-east (February 2000).
- Poor literacy and numeracy skills – the GCSE score of 5 plus grade A*–C was 52 per cent in the south-east versus 38 per cent in the north-east.
- Run-down council estates – 11 per cent of families in the south-west lived in poor housing versus 20 per cent in parts of London and up to 30 per cent in areas of Scotland.
- Death rates are higher in some areas, especially for those in Scotland and Wales. People in these areas will die younger. Glasgow is the city with the highest death rate in Britain.
- A high crime rate and vandalism – some cities in Yorkshire had the highest rate of recorded offences (March 2000).
- Consumer goods – 50 per cent of all households in the south and south-east own a home computer versus 25 per cent in the north-east.

There are of course variations within regions.

- In the north-west, the Lake District has a death rate 46 points below the average, whereas Runcorn is 27 points above (2000).

- Of the top ten poorest local authority areas in England, five are in London.
- Of the top 100 poorest districts in England, 22 are in London.

North-south divide?

No! We now know that the divide is between rich and poor – the 'haves' and 'have-nots'. It is too simple just to divide the UK between north and south.

With ten million people suffering great poverty, it means that about four million children also suffer. People do not listen to children. So children need agencies like the **NSPCC** (National Society for the Prevention of Cruelty to Children) and **CARE** to speak up for them.

Debt and loans

Poor people are at risk from 'loan sharks' who lend money to them to pay off their debts. Then they charge very high interest rates on the repayments. This means the people who have taken out the loan get even more into debt. Pensioners, too, get conned into borrowing against the value of their house, then find they have signed it away.

Solutions

Causes of poverty have been identified, so something can now be done.

- Aim to reduce teenage pregnancies.
- Improve literacy and numeracy skills. Secondary schools offer vocational courses like child care and mechanics. Many offer more worked-based training from Year 9 instead of all academic subjects.
- Money is being spent on housing. For example, housing trusts improve existing housing, and the people have a say in their future.

This is the sort of area that housing trusts can renovate and regenerate.

- Christians who are parish priests or ministers may choose to work with teenagers, or poor families or the elderly. They serve God in practice. They help these people to speak up, get people to listen to their needs and try to get something done.

Activities

1 What are the characteristics of poverty mentioned in this topic? Add any other characteristics you can think of.
   C 2.2, PS 2.1

2 A person wrote to a newspaper: 'The poor people in the UK have only themselves to blame! So stop scrounging money off the state you haven't worked for.'

   a What is your reaction to this? List your thoughts.

   b Do you agree or disagree? Give reasons. **PS 2.1**

Key points

- In the UK, there is a growing problem of a rich-poor divide.
- The actual rich-poor divide is more accurately between areas in the same county or even the same city.

Put an end to child poverty

The Christian Herald, 10 March 2001.

Twelve charities joined together to 'End child poverty' in the UK. Charities involved included Oxfam, NSPCC and The Children's Society. They gave newspapers some facts.

- Over 3 million children in the UK live in extreme poverty.

- Child poverty is here now; it's not a thing of the past.

- Every day charities deal with the results of poverty.

- Poverty causes misery and suffering.

- Child poverty must be the concern of all political parties.

The Children's Society

With children, for children, with you

Cruelty to children must stop. FULL STOP.

Results of child poverty

- One in five children are growing up in a home where no one is employed.

- About 3 million children will go hungry today or not have enough clothing. Many will miss school as they are not dressed properly.

- Many single mums live below the poverty line.

What can be done?

- There must be a national plan.

- There must be a minimum income for families.

- All parents should have access to child care they can afford.

- Poor children should have equal access to education.

- Children should be involved in decision making.

Poverty report

These are things that the inspectors look for when writing their poverty report.

- Poor GCSE exam results.

- Few pupils staying on into the sixth form.

- Poor food and nutrition, leading to poor health.

- Poor housing conditions.

- At least one person unemployed.

Tackling problems

- *Sure Start.* This involves children up to four. It brings together groups to provide help with health and education. It also provides parenting classes for young mothers.

- *New Deal.* This is aimed at getting young people back into work. They receive extra payments to take training or learn 'on the job'.

The Church Army

The Anglican Church trains lay people to become the Church Army. They work with the elderly, young people, drug addicts and alcoholics. They may serve in some of the poorest, most run-down parishes in the roughest towns and cities.

Church Army workers try to involve older people in church planning and activities. They try to change attitudes towards older people.

> 'Many people believe that when you get old you become helpless … People assume that the church can only help the elderly. They don't realize that the elderly can minister to others.'
>
> *Adapted from Church Army Focus Group for Older People.*

Church Army youth workers also work to change attitudes. They understand the stresses of life in the twenty-first century and what it is like to be a teenager.

The Salvation Army

The Salvation Army is an international Christian organization working in 108 countries. It shows God's love by working for the welfare of others. The Salvation Army has over 1.5 million members worldwide. It runs centres for the homeless, schools, hospitals and medical centres. It takes care of pensioners in their own homes.

One carer said: 'We put faith into practice. We promise, for Christ's sake, to care for the poor, feed the hungry, clothe the naked, love the unlovable and befriend the friendless.'

Help the Aged and Age Concern

These two groups often work together for pensioners. They recently persuaded the UK government to reintroduce free eye tests for the elderly. They help pensioners with benefits and pensions claims.

Off to lunch!

Activities

1 Using the Internet, look further into the work of organizations that campaign against poverty. A good place to start your research is the websites of the organisations listed below. To access these websites visit www.heinemann.co.uk/ hotlinks and click on this section.

- Help the Aged
- Salvation Army
- Barnardos **IT 2.1, 2.3**

2 Do you think some people expect too much help from the state? Do you think it should be 'no work, no eat'? List your reasons. **C 2.1a**

3 How do you think ordinary people can help the poorest people? **C 2.1a**

Key points

- The Bible (James) says that you cannot have faith without actions. This is seen in the work of the Salvation Army, Church Army and groups like NSPCC and Help the Aged.

Here you will find the relevant Bible passages that you will need for the aid for developing countries section. The set passages are written out. Then there is an explanation of what they mean.

Set passages

Luke 16: 19–31
(The rich man and Lazarus)

There was a rich man who was dressed in purple and fine linen and lived in luxury every day. At his gate was laid a beggar named Lazarus, covered with sores and longing to eat what fell from the rich man's table …

The time came when the beggar died and the angels carried him to Abraham's side. The rich man also died and was buried. In hell, where he was in torment, he looked up and saw Abraham far away, with Lazarus by his side. So he called to him, 'Father Abraham, have pity on me and send Lazarus to dip the tip of his finger in water and cool my tongue, because I am in agony in this fire.'

But Abraham replied, 'Son, remember that in your lifetime you received your good things, while Lazarus received bad things, but now he is comforted here and you are in agony. And besides all this, between us and you a great chasm has been fixed, so that those who want to go from here to you cannot, nor can anyone cross over from there to us.'

He answered, 'Then I beg you, father, send Lazarus to my father's house, for I have five brothers. Let him warn them, so that they will not also come to this place of torment.'

Abraham replied, 'They have Moses and the Prophets; let them listen to them.' 'No, father Abraham,' he said, 'but if someone from the dead goes to them, they will repent.'

He said to him, 'If they do not listen to Moses and the Prophets, they will not be convinced even if someone rises from the dead.'

The rich man ignored the problem. He could not say he did not know, had not heard or had not been told. We cannot say we do not know what is happening in the world. We have radio and television. We ignore the plight of others at our peril.

Mathew 25: 31–46
(The sheep and the goats)

When the Son of Man comes in his glory, and all the angels with him, he will sit on his throne in heavenly glory. All the nations will be gathered before him, and he will separate the people one from another as a shepherd separates the sheep from the goats. He will put the sheep on his right and the goats on his left.

Then the King will was say to those on his right, 'Come, you who are blessed by my Father; take your inheritance, the kingdom prepared for you since the creation of the world. For I was hungry and you gave me something to eat, I was thirsty and you gave me something to drink, I was a stranger and you invited me in, I needed clothes and you clothed me, I was sick and you looked after me, I was in prison and you came to visit me.'

Then the righteous will answer him, 'Lord, when did we see you hungry and feed you, or thirsty and give you something to drink? When did we see you a stranger and invite you in, or needing clothes and clothe you? When did we see you sick or in prison and go to visit you?'

The King will reply, 'I tell you the truth, whatever you did for one of the least of these brothers of mine, you did for me.'

Then he will say to those on his left, 'Depart from me, you who are cursed, into the eternal fire prepared by the devil and his angels. For I was hungry and you gave me nothing to eat, I was thirsty and you gave me nothing to drink, I was a stranger and you did not invite me in, I needed clothes and you did not clothe me, I was sick and in prison and you did not look after me.'

They also will answer, 'Lord, when did we see you hungry or thirsty or a stranger or needing clothes or sick or in prison, and did not help you?'

He will reply, 'I tell you the truth, whatever you did not do for one of the least of these, you did not do for me.'

Then they will go away to eternal punishment, but the righteous to eternal life.

The sheep stand for the kind people. The goats stand for those who got it wrong. They did not help people in need. Jesus said if you help other people, you are actually helping him.

Note that the six areas of need are just the same as today. And the help needed is the same.

- Hunger   give food
- Thirst   give clean water
- Stranger (a refugee?)   welcome in
- Naked   give clothing
- Sick   take care
- In prison   visit

Agencies like the Salvation Army work in all six areas. Notice that Jesus talks about practical help. There are no conditions laid down and no preaching.

Activities

1 What does the parable in Luke 16: 19–31 teach us about:
   a ignoring a problem in your own town
   b what Christians should do when they hear about someone in need? **C 2.2**

2 Look at the six areas of need in the 'sheep' and the 'goats'. Choose one area and find the name of an agency that helps that need, listing what it does to help. Repeat for each of the other five needs. **IT 2.1, 2.3**

Set passages (cont.)

Luke 12: 13–21 (The rich fool)

Someone in the crowd said to him, 'Teacher, tell my brother to divide the inheritance with me.'

Jesus replied, 'Man, who appointed me a judge or an arbiter between you?' Then he said to them, 'Watch out! Be on your guard against all kinds of greed; a man's life does not consist in the abundance of his possessions.'

And he told them this parable: 'The ground of a certain rich man produced a good crop. He thought to himself, "What shall I do? I have no place to store my crops."

'Then he said, "This is what I'll do. I will tear down my barns and build bigger ones, and there I will store all my grain and my goods. And I'll say to myself, 'You have plenty of good things laid up for many years. Take life easy; eat, drink and be merry.'"

'But God said to him, "You fool! This very night your life will be demanded from you. Then who will get what you have prepared for yourself?" This is how it will be for anyone who stores up things for himself but is not rich towards God.'

The man had everything he needed. But death is equal for everyone. You cannot take anything with you, including wealth. Jesus did not say it was wrong to be rich. What he did say was it matters more to be faithful to God. You cannot predict the future.

Acts 4: 32–37
(Barnabas and the early church)

All the believers were one in heart and mind. No one claimed that any of his possessions was his own, but they shared everything they had. With great power the apostles continued to testify to the resurrection of the Lord Jesus, and much grace was upon them all. There were no needy persons among them. For from time to time those who owned lands or houses sold them, brought the money from the sales and put it at the apostles' feet, and it was distributed to anyone as he had need.

Joseph, a Levite from Cyprus, whom the Apostles called Barnabas (which means Son of Encouragement), sold a field he owned and brought the money and put it at the apostles' feet.

The early Christians put Jesus' words into action. Many Christians lived in communities or groups. The apostles were in charge and everyone shared everything. Barnabas sold a field and gave the money to the apostles so that they could share it out where there was need.

Other relevant passages

Mark 12: 41–44

Jesus sat down opposite the place where the offerings were put and watched the crowd putting their money into the temple treasury. Many rich people threw in large amounts. But a poor widow came and put in two very small copper coins, worth only a fraction of a penny.

Calling his disciples to him, Jesus said, 'I tell you the truth, this poor widow has put more into the treasury than all the others. They gave out of their wealth; but she, out of her poverty, put in everything – all she had to live on.'

Jesus said it does not matter how much or how little you give.

Mark 10: 17–31

A man ran up to Jesus and fell on his knees before him. 'Good teacher,' he asked, 'what must I do to inherit eternal life?'

'Why do you call me good?' Jesus answered. 'No one is good – except God alone. You know the commandments: "Do not murder, do not commit adultery, do not steal, do not give false testimony, do not defraud, honour your father and mother."'

'Teacher,' he declared, 'all these I have kept since I was a boy.'

Jesus looked at him and loved him. 'One thing you lack,' Jesus said. 'Go, sell everything you have and give to the poor, and you will have treasure in heaven. Then come, follow me.'

At this the man's face fell. He went away sad, because he had great wealth.

The disciples were amazed at his words. But Jesus said again, 'Children, how hard it is to enter the kingdom of God! It is easier for a camel to go through the eye of a needle than for a rich man to enter the kingdom of God.'

The disciples were even more amazed, and said to each other, 'Who then can be saved?'

Jesus looked at them and said, 'With man this is impossible, but not with God; all things are possible with God.'

Peter said to him, 'We have left everything to follow you!'

'I tell you the truth,' Jesus replied, 'no one who has left home or brothers or sisters or mother or father or children or fields for me and the gospel will fail to receive a hundred times as much in this present age (homes, brothers, sisters, mothers, children and fields – and with them, persecutions) and in the age to come, eternal life. Many who are first will be last, and the last first.'

Jesus was talking to a rich man who was so near to God's kingdom yet so far from it because his love of wealth stopped his progress. So Jesus went on to explain that wealth can be a hindrance to entering God's kingdom.

The eye of the needle is believed by some to be the small door within the main city gate. A camel loaded with goods would find it almost impossible to get through. The owner would have to unload the camel and get it to crouch down to get it in. (The big gates were rarely opened due to fear of attack.)

1 Timothy 6: 6–10

Godliness without contentment is great gain. For we brought nothing into the world, and we can take nothing out of it. But if we have food and clothing, we will be content with that. People who want to get rich fall into temptation and a trap and into many foolish and harmful desires that plunge men into ruin and destruction. For the love of money is a root of all kinds of evil. Some people, eager for money, have wandered from the faith and pierced themselves with many griefs.

Paul warns that if you desire money all the time it will take over your life and lead to other things like theft.

Activities

1 Explain one point that Jesus taught about wealth. **C 1.2, 2.2**

2 Explain in your own words why Jesus said it is harder for the rich to enter God's kingdom than the poor. Do you think Jesus is right? Give reasons. **PS 1.1**

3 What do you think 'The love of money is the root all evil' means? **PS 1.1**

Exam questions to practise

Below are some sample exam questions from paper 2A. To help you score full marks, the first three questions are followed by some tips from examiners. Before attempting the remaining two questions, try to work out your own method for approaching them.

1 'There in a crisis, there in the long term.' What is this slogan saying about the types of aid given to a developing country? Give some specific examples from the agency which you have studied. (6) *(AQA 2002)*

2 Give one reason why a developing country is poor. (3)
(NEAB 2000, B5aii)

3 A Christian Aid slogan says: 'We believe in life before death.'
 a Explain what this slogan means. (3)

 b Give one example of how these words might be put into action. (2)
(based on NEAB 1999)

Now try questions 4 and 5 on your own. Before you write your answers, spend some time thinking about your approach.

4 'Christians should never get tired of helping the poor.' Do you agree? Give reasons showing you have thought about more than one point of view. Refer to one Bible passage. (5)
(based on NEAB 1997)

5 Explain why Christians are often found in developing countries helping those in need. Refer to one Bible passage. (4) *(NEAB 2000, B5c)*

How to do well

1 Read the slogan carefully. Think about the two types of aid given. Use at least one example from your study of an agency for each type of aid.

2 Only one reason is asked for. You will not gain extra marks for two reasons. You will gain one mark for the reason, and two for explaining it clearly.

3 Is there a Christian belief that sounds like the slogan?
 a Explain what Christians believe about helping the poor.
 b The example should be taken from one of the four agencies you have studied.

Coursework

Coursework is an essential part of the GCSE examination

For the GCSE full course, candidates must submit two assignments of between 1000–1500 words, one for each option taken. This book covers one option.

Your coursework must show the following.

- What you *know* about Christian attitudes to moral issues, and how faith has affected what people believe and do. (Knowledge)

- That you can explain what Christians believe and how these beliefs affect the way they live and worship. (Understanding)

- That you can give *your own opinion* and show other points of view (Evaluation)

Knowledge

Do not write down everything you can find out! You need to show that you can select *relevant* information that answers the question. For example, if the task is 'Explain the purposes of Christian marriage', then you should do the following.

- Decide what the question really means. Here it means, 'Why do Christians get married?'

- The introduction to the Wedding ceremony in the Anglican Church gives good information about this.

- For each point you need to explain what it means, and give examples –including Bible passages and other Christian teaching. So, for example, you may want to explain why Christians believe marriage is the right place for sex. Who says so? Why?

Understanding

This part is to show you understand the information you are writing down. For example, a Christian may or may not fight in a war. You must show you understand:

- key words and their meaning – for example, 'pacifist'.

- people's feelings and emotions – for example, protecting their family.

Evaluation

Here you must give your own opinion. But you must also show you understand more than one point of view. You can give one for and one against the quotation. For example, a question might be: 'Do you agree with the statement "Capital punishment is the only suitable punishment for a murderer."' You must refer to Christianity in your answer and show you have considered more than one point of view.

- First you need to give at least one view that supports (agrees with) this statement. You could quote the Old Testament view on fair punishment 'An eye for an eye'. Then explain what this means and add other references.

- Give at least one view against the statement. You might write how Jesus spoke about forgiveness, not revenge. You could then move on to the idea of reform.

- Do not criticize the views of others. For example, you must not write 'That's a stupid point of view.'

- Finally, make it clear what you think. You will not gain full marks if you only give one point of view. You will also fail to gain full marks if you do not state your own point of view.

Writing your assignment

Before you begin

Read the whole question several times and ask yourself:

- What is the whole assignment about?

- What information have I already got (for example, class notes)?

- What must I find out? How will I do that?

- Do I need to go somewhere – for example, a church?

Information

Books

- Only use books that you understand.

- Keep to the point.

- Do not copy large chunks.

- If you quote from a book, put it in inverted commas.

- In the bibliography and coursework cover sheet you must note all books used giving the title, author and publisher.

- Suitable quotes could be, for example, a few verses from the Bible, or part of someone's speech.

Internet

- There are no extra marks for using the Internet.

- Do not copy (download) large chunks from the Internet.

- Websites sometimes hold irrelevant information, so be aware of this. Only write what you understand.

- In the bibliography and cover sheet you must write down the full website address (for example, www …) and the title of the article.

Interviews

- Decide carefully who you want to interview and why (for example, a soldier).

- If everyone wants to interview the same person, then it may be better to invite that person to your class. Your teacher may help.

- Decide beforehand exactly what questions you will ask.

- Before the interview let the person you are interviewing know what questions you are going to ask.

Surveys

These can be useful, but you must go prepared.

- What are you trying to find out?

- How will you record responses? Ticks? Writing down an answer?

- Decide how many people you wish to interview and where. Do you need permission first? For example, if you interview people going to church, you should tell the vicar first.

- You will need clipboard and pens.

- How will you show your findings?

Your coursework

- If you are unsure about anything, before and during the assignment, ASK YOUR TEACHER.

- Check spelling, punctuation and grammar. If you use a computer to do this, set it to UK spellings (not US).

- Remember, this work is about a moral issue seen from a Christian point of view.

- If a page goes wrong, then start again!

- Begin each part of the question on a separate piece of paper.

- Only number the pages once you have finished, in case you need to add something.

- Try to use the correct religious terms – for example, 'Jesus taught using parables.' Don't write, 'Jesus taught using stories.'

- Try to use the correct vocabulary – for example, use the word 'pacifist' rather than saying 'the person disagrees with any violence'.

Finished!

- Read the finished assignment at least twice. Check you have answered all parts of the question. If there is an error, it may be best to begin again.

- Do not forget to check you have noted down all books and websites that you have used.

- Count the number of words – there are no extra marks if you go over.

The following websites will help you to find out more about some of the issues covered in this book. To access the sites please visit www.heinemann.co.uk/hotlinks and click on this section.

ACLU (American Civil Liberties Union)
Campaigns against the death penalty.

Amnesty International
Campaigns on behalf of prisoners worldwide, especially those imprisoned without trial.

Archbishop Desmond Tutu
Spiritual leader of South Africa, opposed to apartheid. He chose non-violent protest.

Archbishop Oscar Romero
The archbishop of San Salvador, El Salvador. He spoke up for the poor.

CAFOD (Catholic Fund for Overseas Development)
A Roman Catholic Agency that supports projects run locally in developing countries.

Christian Aid
Supports projects in developing countries, and co-ordinates joint projects and appeals with other agencies.

CND (Campaign for Nuclear Disarmament)
Founded in 1958, campaigns against nuclear bombs.

CRE (Commission for Racial Equality)
Deals with cases of racial discrimination.

Dietrich Bonhoeffer
German pacifist pastor who joined resistance to Nazi rule.

Environment Agency
The governmental department that looks after the environment.

EXIT
A voluntary euthanasia supporters group.

Greenpeace
An international group that aims to protect the world.

Groundwork Trust
An organization that undertakes environmental projects in the local community.

LIFE
A society that believes life begins at conception and that all life should be equally protected by law. It provides practical help and advice.

Marie Stopes International
Gives advice on all issues connected with contraception and pregnancy (including abortion).

Marriage Care
Aims to show compassion and help people sort out marriage problems.

Martin Luther King
Leader of the black Americans in the 1950s and 1960s. He advocated peaceful protests to gain basic human rights for black people.

Nelson Mandela
Former leader of the ANC in South Africa. After many years in prison, he became president of South Africa in 1994. He retired in 2000.

Positive parenting
Provides positive alternatives to parenting methods such as smacking.

Relate
Offers marriage and relationship guidance. Also provides family counselling.

Saint Maximilian Kolbe
A Polish priest sent to a concentration camp. He took the place of another prisoner condemned to starve to death.

SPUC (Society for the Protection of the Unborn Child)
The first group to be called pro-life. It aims to protect human life from conception to birth.

Tearfund
Aid agency working world-wide to support locally run projects.

Trócaire
A Roman Catholic Agency supported by the Irish government. It works in developing countries and war zones such as Kosovo.

WHO (World Health Organization)
Concerned with health world-wide. It helps governments to set up health systems.

Glossary

Abortion Operation to terminate (end) a pregnancy before the foetus can live.

Absolution Being released from a sin by a priest.

Acupuncture Ancient Chinese medical treatment to help natural healing. Needles are inserted into special points in the body. Western acupuncture is usually used to relieve pain.

Adultery Sex between a married man or woman and someone to whom they are not married.

Aid Help sent to countries in need either in an emergency or over the long-term.

AIDS Acquired Immune Deficiency Syndrome. A virus called HIV destroys the body's immune system. The virus is passed between people by contact with blood or semen.

Aim of punishment The reason for the choice of punishment. The intended outcome.

ANC (African National Congress) The main opposition group in South Africa during late twentieth century. Led by Nelson Mandela.

Annulment Cancelling a marriage as though it never existed.

Apartheid Policy of South African government to separate the white and black populations. Black people were treated as inferior.

Apostle Greek, meaning 'sent out'. One of twelve special followers who Jesus chose to take his message to the people.

Assisted suicide A patient requests help to die from another person. A form of voluntary euthanasia.

Banns Announcement in church that two people intend to marry each other.

Baptism The act of sprinkling, pouring or immersing in water. This is part of becoming a Christian.

Betrothal Promise to marry someone. Engagement.

Big Bang theory Theory about the creation of the universe. This came about when a huge explosion happened 15,000 million years ago.

Boycott To refuse to deal with or buy from a person or country.

Capital punishment A criminal is punished by death.

CARE Christian Action Research. An organization that aims to protect families, the elderly and children.

Casual sex Sex without commitment.

Catechism Teaching Christian belief by using questions and answers.

Catholic 'Universal' or 'worldwide'. The church is not limited to one country or one race of people.

Cavalry Part of the army that fights on horseback.

Celibacy Choosing not to have sex for a particular reason.

CFCs Chlorofluorocarbon. A gas which is now banned because it destroys the ozone layer.

Chastity Sexual purity.

Chinese herbs Traditional Chinese medicine.

Civil war War between citizens of the same country.

Civil wedding The couple do not marry in church. They have a non-religious service in a registry office or place licensed for weddings.

Civilian A person who is not military.

Compassion Strong feeling of sympathy for someone who is suffering.

Conception The point at which a woman becomes pregnant.

Conscientious objector Person who refuses to fight in a war on grounds of conscience.

Consecrate To make holy.

Conservation Looking after the environment and the world we live in.

Contagious Illness that can be caught by touching.

Corrupt Dishonest. Using position or power to commit crimes. Open to bribery.

Creed From the Latin 'credo' ('I believe'). A summary of Christian belief.

Crime Breaking the law of the land – for example, stealing.

Crusades Military expeditions by Christian armies in eleventh to thirteenth centuries to recover the Holy Land from the Muslims.

Death Row Section of prison where those sentenced to death are kept.

Debt Money owed by individuals or countries.

Delegation Group of people sent to a conference on behalf of someone else or a country.

Denomination A group of churches with the same beliefs and traditions – for example, Anglican, Roman Catholic, Baptist.

Desolate Empty, bare.

Developing country A poor country, lacking technology, usually in parts of Africa, South America and the Middle East. Formerly known as 'third world'.

Devout Very religious.

Dictator A non-elected leader of a country who has total power.

Dignity A composed manner.

Disarmament Getting rid of weapons.

Discrimination Treating people unfairly on account of, for example, gender, race or age.

Disease Illness that may cause early death or disability.

Divorce The legal ending of a marriage.

Environment The natural world in which animals, including humans, live.

Ethnic minority Group of people of a particular race or nationality that is different from the majority of people living in that country.

Euthanasia 'Easy death.' Ending the life of someone who is ill at the request of the sick person or with the consent of their family.

Evangelical churches Churches that focus on spreading the Good News to non-Christians. Their services are often outgoing and lively.

Evolution Development of species from early forms, gradually changing to adapt to the environment.

Extinct Died out, no longer existing.

Fidelity Faithfulness.

Fornication Sexual activity outside marriage. Includes sex before marriage.

Fossils Remains or impression of animal or plant preserved in rock.

Freedom fighters Another name for terrorists.

Fundamental 'Basic', as in Christians who want to 'get back to basic' teachings of Christianity.

G8 countries USA, Canada, Japan, France, UK, Germany, Italy and Russia. They meet annually to discuss world issues.

General Synod The ruling body of the Church of England. It is made up of bishops, clergy and elected lay people.

Genesis 'Beginnings.' The first book of the Bible.

Gentile Someone who is not a Jew.

Gospel 'Good News.' The Gospels of Matthew, Mark, Luke and John tell the life story of Jesus.

Green issues Issues concerning the care of the world, the environment.

Habitat Natural home of an animal, plant, insect or other living thing.

HIV/HIV positive *See AIDS*.

Holy Communion Also called the Mass, the Eucharist, the Lord's Supper. It remembers Jesus' last meal with his apostles when he said the bread and wine were symbols of his body and blood.

Holy Spirit Third person of the Trinity. God sends the Holy Spirit to Christians to guide and inspire them.

Holy war War fought in the belief that God is on their side.

Homeopathy Medical treatment using small doses of natural substances that would produce symptoms of the illness. Known as 'treating like with like'.

Homosexual Someone who has sexual affection for a person of the same sex.

Hospice A home for the care of the terminally ill.

Humane Kind. Making sure that a person or animal does not suffer.

Illiterate Unable to read or write.

Inhumane Unkind, cruel.

Just war War that a Christian believes has a right cause and can be justified.

Kingdom of God God ruling in the world.

Kosher Foods allowed by Jewish dietary laws.

Leper Someone who suffers from leprosy, an infectious disease. It causes disfigurement and disability. In earlier times, lepers became social outcasts.

Literalists People who believe the Bible means exactly what it says, and is not open to interpretation.

Living will A patient's written intention to enable him or her to refuse unwanted treatment, even if he or she cannot say so due to coma. It may be to refuse antibiotics or being linked to a life-support system.

Long-term aid Aid spread over many years with the goal of enabling a country to become self-reliant.

Malnutrition Not having a balanced, regular diet.

Marriage The state of being joined as husband and wife.

Martyr Person who is prepared to die for his or her beliefs.

Mass *See Holy Communion*.

Media TV, radio, newspapers, etc. Those who communicate with the public.

Mercy killing *See Assisted suicide*.

Montreal protocol International agreement to protect the ozone layer. It agreed that CFCs and other toxic substances would be phased out by 2005.

Myth A story with imaginary people, objects and animals to try to explain how natural events came about – for example, the Creation.

Nationalism/Nationalist Extreme form of love for one's country. Sometimes involves the wish to exclude or remove some minority groups. Also, may include desire for independence for a region.

NATO (North Atlantic Treaty Organization) An international organization made up of the USA, Canada, Iceland, Britain and fifteen European countries. NATO aims to protect its members and provides troops to keep the peace.

NHS (National Health Service) Provides free health care throughout the UK.

Nicene Creed A statement of Christian beliefs, agreed at the Council of Nicaea in AD 325.

Non-violent protest Peaceful protest, using sit-ins or boycotts. Sometimes those sent to break up the protest use violence.

NSPCC (National Society for the Prevention of Cruelty to Children) Tries to stop abuse, cruelty and neglect towards children.

Nuclear weapons Also called hydrogen bomb or atom bomb. The explosion causes mass destruction and radioactive fall-out.

Nurture To care for and bring up a child.

Organic farmers Farmers who do not use harmful chemicals to grow food.

Orthodox Church Main church in Greece and Russia. Orthodox means traditional.

Ozone layer A layer of gas above the earth that is being destroyed by CFCs.

Pacifist A person who believes all wars and all fighting are wrong.

Patriotism/Patriotic Love for one's country. Usually accompanied by resistance to change.

Pollution Something that causes the environment to become foul.

Poverty cycle Also called the poverty trap. People who are poor have no education, get low-paid jobs and cannot get out of the cycle.

Prejudice Having a biased, unfair attitude about a person or group without getting to know them.

Primary health care Health care aimed at preventing disease.

Prisoners of conscience People in prison for their political or religious beliefs.

Pro-choice Belief that a woman has the right to choose whether or not to have an abortion.

Pro-life Belief that a foetus is a living human being from the moment of conception. This means the foetus has full right to life and abortion is the same as murder.

Reconciliation To bring friends back together. For Christians, to bring a person back to God.

Refugees People who leave their own country and cross into another country to escape war or religious/racial persecution.

Remarriage Getting married again to a different partner. This may be following a death, or after divorce or annulment.

Repentance (penitence) To be sorry for wrongdoing and to try to put things right.

Resistance group/movement Secret group opposed to the Nazis in France and other occupied countries in World War II.

Sacrament 'The outward sign of an inward grace.' A sign of something sacred or holy. Baptism and Holy Communion are sacraments that Jesus began.

Sanctity of life A belief that human life is sacred, or holy, and must be respected.

Segregation A split or separation between groups of people.

Sexism Discrimination or unfair treatment based on gender.

Shanty town An area of housing that is makeshift, made from recycled materials. There may be no sanitation or clean water.

Short-term aid Emergency aid sent in response to a disaster such as hurricane or flood.

Sin Breaking God's law in thought or action, or in good work left undone.

Social Services A department of local councils in the UK providing help and care for families, the elderly, children, disabled people and the sick.

Spouse Husband or wife.

Stewardship Looking after something for someone else. In this book it means looking after the world on behalf of God.

Suicide The act of killing yourself.

Tenakh The Hebrew Bible. Jewish scriptures.

TENS machine A machine developed to relieve pain. It has electrical pads that send impulses to damaged nerves. This means the patient can avoid having to take drugs.

Terrorism Use of threats or violence to create fear in a population. The aim is to bring about political change.

Theology The study of religion and religious beliefs.

Tithing/Tithe Giving one-tenth of your income back to God. In past times, it was based on produce and animals.

Traumatic A shock, often emotional.

Tyrant A ruler with complete power over his people, who uses it unfairly and cruelly.

United Nations (UN) An organization of countries of the world that meet to discuss world issues such as Human Rights.

Vaccination An injection to protect against infectious diseases such as measles.

Voluntary euthanasia If a patient is dying and in great pain, he or she may ask to be allowed to die. They may ask someone to help them die. *See also Assisted suicide.*

Vows Solemn promises, especially those in marriage or ordination.

War Armed conflict between two or more opposing groups.

Weapons of mass destruction Nuclear and chemical weapons that kill thousands of people at once. Effects may be long-term, such as radioactive contamination.

Wedding The marriage ceremony.

Yoga An ancient Hindu art. It is meditation combined with physical and mental exercises. It can help people who suffer with stress.

Youth Offending Teams (YOTs) Local authorities in the UK set these up with the aim of identifying young people who commit crime and helping to prevent crime.

Index

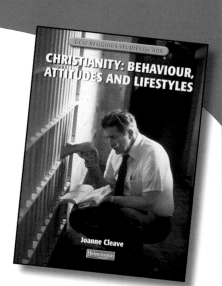
 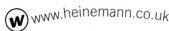